C000002158

KS2 SATs
Maths
Revision Guide

Hilary Koll and Steve Mills

Schofield & Sims

Welcome to this book

This book will help you revise for the national tests in maths at the end of Key Stage 2.

Red headings show you which topic is covered.

Illustrations and diagrams help you to understand the topic.

This tells you which page can help you with this topic.

Find out about words in **bold** by turning to the Glossary.

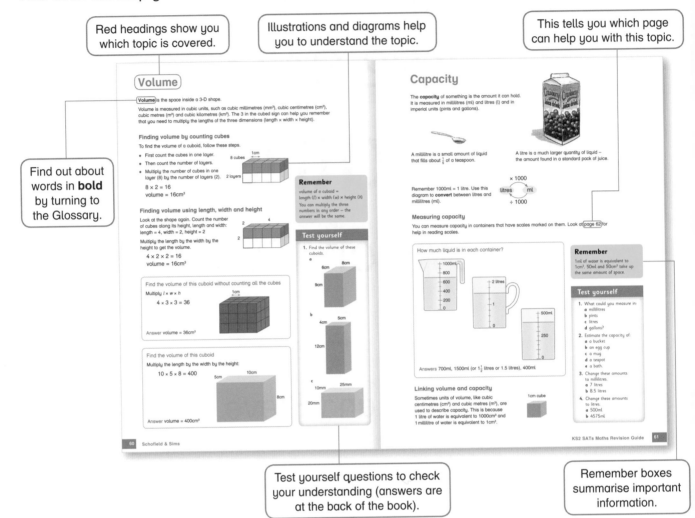

Test yourself questions to check your understanding (answers are at the back of the book).

Remember boxes summarise important information.

How to revise

● Turn to the topic and read about it.

● Read the Remember box and then cover it up. Can you remember what it says?

● Read the Test yourself questions and write your answers on a piece of paper.

● Check your answers against the right answers at the back of the book.

● If you got any answers wrong, read the topic again, then have another go at the questions.

● If you got the answers right – well done! Move on to the next topic.

● Once you have worked through this revision guide, move on to the maths papers in the **KS2 SATs Maths and English Practice Papers**.

Tips for tests

● Always read the question carefully before you answer it.

● Have a go at as many questions as you can. If there is a question you really can't answer, just move on to the next one. You can always come back to it if you have time.

● Always approximate before you calculate. Check your calculations by doing them a different way, using an inverse operation and by using your approximation.

● If you have time at the end, check through your work.

Contents

Place value

There are 10 digits.

You can put these digits together to make numbers. For example, 274 is a three-digit number and 3092764 is a seven-digit number.

Look at this number ⟶ 4 5 1 5 2

The digit 5 appears twice, but its value each time is very different.

5000   50

The position of a digit in a number gives its value. If you are not sure how large a number is, write the headings over the digits.

Look at the number 45152

	Ten Thousands	Thousands	Hundreds	Tens	Ones
You write the number in full like this ⟶	4 ↓ 40000	+	5 ↓ 5000	+	1 ↓ 100	+	5 ↓ 50	+	2 ↓ 2

Now look at the number 7328436

	Millions	Hundred Thousands	Ten Thousands	Thousands	Hundreds	Tens	Ones
You write the number in full like this ⟶	7 ↓ 7000000	+ 3 ↓ 300000	+ 2 ↓ 20000	+ 8 ↓ 8000	+ 4 ↓ 400	+ 3 ↓ 30	+ 6 ↓ 6

Zeros are important because they keep other digits in their proper places. The number 505 without a zero would be just 55. And 30500 would be only 35.

Test yourself

1. Write these in full. The first one has been done for you.
   a 312 = 300 + 10 + 2   **b** 4839   **c** 69215   **d** 2106387

2. Write the value of the blue digit in each number.
   a 702   **d** 529573
   b 3028   **e** 275003
   c 41256   **f** 2800645

Remember

These are the digit headings:

Millions, Hundred Thousands, Ten Thousands, Thousands, Hundreds, Tens, Ones.

Writing numbers in words

You can use the digit headings to help you write numbers in words.

Write 3784 in words

	Thousands	Hundreds	Tens	Ones
3784 ——→	3	7	8	4

Answer three thousand, seven hundred and eighty-four

Write 52009 in words

	Ten Thousands	Thousands	Hundreds	Tens	Ones
52009 ——→	5	2	0	0	9

Answer fifty-two thousand and nine

Write 721936 in words

	Hundred Thousands	Ten Thousands	Thousands	Hundreds	Tens	Ones
721936 ——→	7	2	1	9	3	6

Answer seven hundred and twenty-one thousand, nine hundred and thirty-six

---

Large numbers

Very large numbers can be grouped in threes from the right, like this.

31 670 432 ——→ thirty-one million, six hundred and seventy thousand, four hundred and thirty-two

As numbers like this are so large, we often leave spaces to make them easier to read.

54 893 091

Adding and subtracting

Make sure you know the values of the numbers you are adding and subtracting, so that you add tens to tens, hundreds to hundreds, and so on.

This sum was incorrectly set out and has been corrected.

```
  2 5 7 9 1 9 3   ✗        2 5 7 9 1 9 3   ✓
+ 5 3 7 0 4            +       5 3 7 0 4
```

Test yourself

1. Write these numbers in words.
   a 351   **b** 4857   **c** 2041   **d** 50091   **e** 659234   **f** 2437896

2. Write these numbers using digits.
   a five thousand, two hundred and fifty-four
   b sixty-one thousand, five hundred and ninety-one
   c six million, five hundred and four thousand, three hundred and eight

Remember

Line up the digits correctly when adding and subtracting numbers.

Rounding

You sometimes need to round numbers to give a quick idea of a number. Which do you think is the better of these two headlines?

MAN WINS A MILLION POUNDS!

Man wins nine hundred and sixty-two thousand, five hundred and twelve pounds fifty-seven pence!

Rounding will also give a rough answer before you **calculate**.

43×18 is about the same as $40 \times 20 = 800$

The words 'round' or 'approximate' in maths are usually followed by the words 'to the nearest'. To round numbers, you must decide what you are rounding to.

The number 1 766 259 could be rounded to...

the nearest 10	⟶	1 766 260
the nearest 100	⟶	1 766 300
the nearest 1000	⟶	1 766 000
the nearest 10 000	⟶	1 770 000
the nearest 100 000	⟶	1 800 000
the nearest 1 000 000	⟶	2 000 000

Rounding with a number line

One way of rounding is to look at the number on a number line and see which **multiple** of the number you are rounding to it is nearest to. For example, if you are rounding to the nearest 100, look to see which mulitple of 100 the number is nearest to.

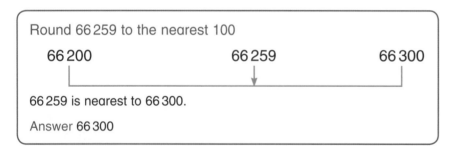

Round 66 259 to the nearest 100

66 200   66 259   66 300

66 259 is nearest to 66 300.

Answer 66 300

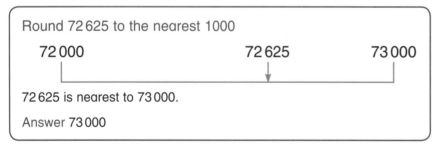

Round 72 625 to the nearest 1000

72 000   72 625   73 000

72 625 is nearest to 73 000.

Answer 73 000

Rounding without a number line

A second way of doing this is to see what you are rounding to (here, it is to the nearest 100).
Then point to this digit in the number.

TTh	Th	H	T	O
6	6	2	5	9

Look at the digit to the right of it.

6	6	2	<u>5</u>	9

If it's smaller than 5, the digit stays the same. If it's 5 or larger, the digit goes up one.

Zeros then cover the digits to the right.

6	6	3	<u>0</u>	<u>0</u>

Round 6 723 769 to the nearest 100

M	HTh	TTh	Th	H	T	O
6	7	2	3	7	6	9

Point to the 100 digit. Look to the right.
6 is more than 5. So the digit 7 needs to go up
one. Zeros cover the digits to the right.

Answer 6 723 800

Round 2 497 286 to the nearest 1000

M	HTh	TTh	Th	H	T	O
2	4	9	7	2	8	6

Point to the 1000 digit. Look to the right.
2 is less than 5. So the digit 7 stays the same.
Zeros cover the digits to the right.

Answer 2 497 000

If your digit is a 9 and it needs to go up one, change it to zero and add one to the digit on its left instead.

Round 6 709 728 to the nearest 1000

6 709 728 becomes 6 710 000

Answer 6 710 000

Round 3 986 473 to the nearest 100 000

3 986 473 becomes 4 000 000

Answer 4 000 000

Rounding decimals

You can round decimals in exactly the same way as whole numbers.

For more information on decimals, see page 24. Rounding decimals is covered on page 26.

Test yourself

1. Round these numbers to the nearest 10.
   a 2419   b 3504   c 5427   d 6499

2. Round these numbers to the nearest 100.
   a 2891   b 8629   c 9045   d 62 981

3. Round these numbers to the nearest 1000.
   a 62 194   b 45 091   c 74 999   d 39 522

4. Round these numbers to the nearest 10 000, then to the nearest
   100 000, then to the nearest 1 000 000.
   a 4 737 924   b 2 893 562   c 6 185 057

Remember

Use rounding to check your
answers. Always check what
you are rounding to, such as the
nearest 1000, 10 000 or 100 000.

Ordering and comparing numbers

When ordering and comparing numbers, make sure you know the value of each digit (see pages 4–5).

Which of these cities has the largest population, next largest and so on?

London	9 126 524
Paris	2 141 483
St Petersburg	5 381 736
Rome	2 857 321
Bucharest	2 106 144

Think about the digit headings. When the numbers have the same number of digits, ask the following.

Which number has most millions? 9 126 524

Which has the next greatest number of millions? 5 381 736

Which numbers have the next greatest number of millions? 2 141 483 2 857 321 2 106 144

Which of these has most hundreds of thousands? 2 857 321

Which numbers have the next greatest number of hundreds of thousands? 2 141 483 2 106 144

Which of these has the greatest number of tens of thousands? 2 141 483

Which is the smallest number? 2 106 144

Answer	London	9 126 524
	St Petersburg	5 381 736
	Rome	2 857 321
	Paris	2 141 483
	Bucharest	2 106 144

Finding a number between two others

Give a number between 23 854 and 23 671

- Compare the two numbers. They both have '23 thousand', so your answer will too.
- Compare the other digits: 854 and 671

You need to write a number that is larger than 23 671 but smaller than 23 854.

Answer (examples) 23 672, 23 700 or 23 800

Finding a number halfway between two others

What number is halfway between 2346 and 2142?
- Find the difference between the numbers: 2346 − 2142 = 204
- Halve the answer. Half of 204 is 102.
- Add 102 to the smaller number: 2142

Answer 2244

Another (quicker) way is to add the two numbers together and halve the answer.

Test yourself

1. Order these numbers, largest first.
   6291   92 716   80 062   8502   67 293

2. Order these numbers, smallest first.
   54 351   48 602   51 762   48 701   50 001

3. Order these numbers, smallest first.
   3 461 590   3 946 724   3 491 042   3 493 533   3 163 067

4. Write the number that is halfway between 3482 and 3164.

Remember

To find the number halfway between two others:

- find the difference, halve it and add it to the smaller number
- or, add the two numbers and halve the answer.

Positive and negative numbers

Negative numbers

A **negative number** is a number that is less than zero. Negative numbers have a minus sign in front of them, like −8 and −1, to show how many less than 0 they are.

Temperature

One use of negative numbers is to show temperature. Look at this thermometer.

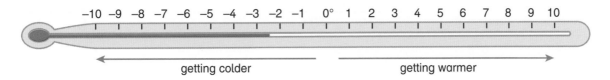

When the temperature falls below zero degrees Celsius (0°C), you use negative numbers. They show how far below zero it is.

On the thermometer you can see that −3° is colder than 0°, and −5° is colder than −2°. On this thermometer, the temperature further to the left is always colder.

Number lines

This number line also shows negative numbers. Use the number line to see why −3 is smaller than 0, and −5 is smaller than −2.

Find −3 and 0 on the line. The number further to the left is always smaller. Find −2 and −5 on the line. −5 is smaller than −2.

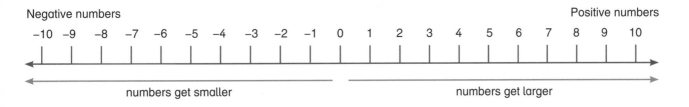

This is only part of the number line − it goes on forever in both directions.

Positive numbers

Positive numbers are the numbers we use every day, like 12, 27 and 100. You can put a + sign in front of them, like +12 and +27, but this usually isn't necessary.

Positive and negative numbers are used in lots of real-life situations, from songs moving up or down the music charts, to showing distances above and below sea level.

Test yourself

1. In these pairs, which is the smaller number?
   a 8, 3   c −9, 2   e −14, −9
   b 4, −2   d −5, −2   f −5, −10

Remember

Negative numbers are less than zero, positive numbers are greater than zero. −6 is smaller than −5 even though with positive numbers 6 is larger than 5.

Number lines

You can use a number line to order numbers.

Put –2, 8, 3, 0, –10, –6 in order of size, starting with the smallest

Place each number on the line, like this:

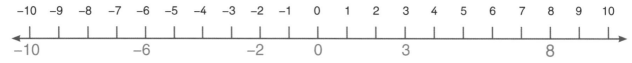

Negative numbers · Positive numbers

-10 -9 -8 -7 -6 -5 -4 -3 -2 -1 0 1 2 3 4 5 6 7 8 9 10

-10 · -6 · -2 · 0 · 3 · 8

Answer –10, –6, –2, 0, 3, 8

Put 7, –1, –3, 10, –8, –5 in order of size, starting with the largest

Place each number on the line, like this:

Negative numbers · Positive numbers

-10 -9 -8 -7 -6 -5 -4 -3 -2 -1 0 1 2 3 4 5 6 7 8 9 10

-8 · -5 · -3 · -1 · 7 · 10

Answer 10, 7, –1, –3, –5, –8

Finding the difference between numbers

At 10 a.m. the temperature outside was –10°C. At 4 p.m. it was –2°C.
What was the difference in temperatures?

Find the numbers on the line. Count from one to the other (count the jumps, not the marks!).

Negative numbers

-10 -9 -8 -7 -6 -5 -4 -3 -2 -1 0 1 2 3 4 5 6 7 8 9 10

8 places to the left

Answer The difference was 8°C.

Test yourself

1. Put these numbers in order. Start with the smallest.
   a 6, –2, 4, 0, 7   c –4, 4, –7, –2, 10   e –1, –12, –54, –23, –6
   b 2, –9, 4, 3, –1   d –5, –2, –15, 7, –1

2. a At 6 a.m. the temperature was –9°C. At 2 p.m. it was –1°C.
      What was the difference in temperatures?
   b At noon the temperature was 8°C. At midnight it was –5°C.
      What was the difference in temperatures?

Remember

Draw a number line when ordering or finding the difference between temperatures.

Find the difference between 2 and –3

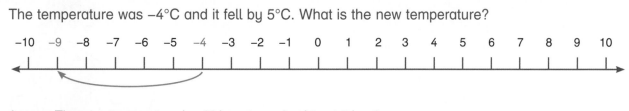

Negative numbers   Positive numbers

–10 –9 –8 –7 –6 –5 –4 –3 –2 –1   0   1   2   3   4   5   6   7   8   9 10

Answer There is a difference of 5 places, so the difference is 5.

To subtract a **positive number** from a **negative number**, start at the first number and count along the number line to the left. Use this method to find temperature falls.

The temperature was –4°C and it fell by 5°C. What is the new temperature?

–10 –9 –8 –7 –6 –5 –4 –3 –2 –1   0   1   2   3   4   5   6   7   8   9 10

Answer The new temperature is –9° because –4 subtract 5 is –9.

When counting, use zero as a 'stepping stone', as below.

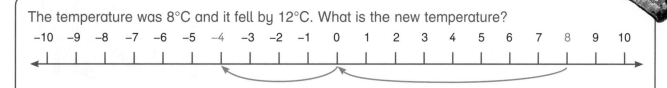

The temperature was 8°C and it fell by 12°C. What is the new temperature?

–10 –9 –8 –7 –6 –5 –4 –3 –2 –1   0   1   2   3   4   5   6   7   8   9 10

Answer 4 places + 8 places = 12 places, so the new temperature is –4°.

Adding positive and negative numbers

To add positive and negative numbers, start at the first number and count along the number line to the right. Use this method to find temperature rises.

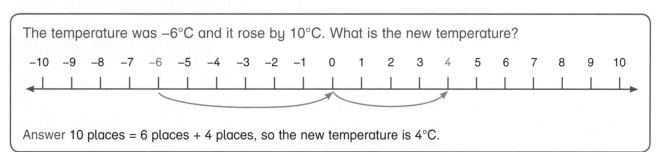

The temperature was –6°C and it rose by 10°C. What is the new temperature?

–10 –9 –8 –7 –6 –5 –4 –3 –2 –1   0   1   2   3   4   5   6   7   8   9 10

Answer 10 places = 6 places + 4 places, so the new temperature is 4°C.

Test yourself

1. Find the difference between:
   a 3 and –4   b 5 and –7   c –3 and 6   d –4 and –9   e –1 and –10
2. Use a number line to solve these.
   a –4 – 3   b –2 – 6   c –1 – 7   d –8 – 3   e –6 – 6   f –2 – 10
3. Use a number line to solve these.
   a –5 + 4   b –3 + 2   c –4 + 8   d –2 + 9   e –5 + 7   f –6 + 4

Remember

Think of temperature rises as + and temperature falls as –.

Use a number line like this:

• when subtracting, move to the left

• when adding, move to the right.

Number sequences

You can continue number **sequences** by finding the difference between **adjacent** numbers. Subtract or count on from the smaller number.

Continue the sequence 5 12 19 26 33 40 ___

In this sequence, the 'difference number' is the same:

So the next number is 40 + 7

Answer 47

Continue the sequence 37 29 22 16 11 7 ___

In this sequence, there is a different kind of pattern:

So the next number is 7 − 3

Answer 4

Explaining a number sequence

When you are asked to explain a number sequence or pattern:
- use numbers in your explanation
- use words like 'difference', 'larger', smaller', 'decreasing', 'increasing', '**descending**' and '**ascending**'.

Explain this pattern: 8 13 18 23 28

Answer The first number is 8. The numbers in this sequence get larger by a difference of 5 each time.

Now explain this pattern: 5 6 8 11 15

Answer The first number is 5. The difference between each number in this sequence increases by 1 each time. The difference goes 1, 2, 3, 4, and so on.

Remember

Explain sequences using numbers to describe the differences and words like increasing, ascending, decreasing, descending, and so on.

Test yourself

1. Write down the next three numbers.
   a 4 11 18 25 ___ ___ ___
   b 7 16 25 34 ___ ___ ___
   c 41 35 29 23 ___ ___ ___
   d 56 43 30 17 ___ ___ ___

2. Write down the next three numbers.
   a 5 7 10 14 ___ ___ ___
   b 7 9 13 19 ___ ___ ___
   c 32 29 25 20 ___ ___ ___
   d 100 89 79 70 ___ ___ ___

3. Explain in words each of the patterns in the questions above.

Missing numbers in a linear sequence

Look at this **linear sequence**.

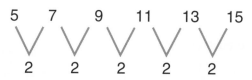

Now imagine you are given only the first and last numbers and have to find the missing ones.

- Find the difference between 5 and 15: it's 10.
- Count the gaps between the two numbers. There are 5 gaps.
- 10 ÷ 5 = 2 so each number is 2 more than the one before.

Make sure you count the number of gaps and not the amount of missing numbers!

> Fill in the missing numbers in this sequence
>
> 4 ___ ___ ___ ___ 19
>
> The difference between 4 and 19 is 15 and there are 5 gaps.
>
> 15 ÷ 5 = 3, so each number is 3 more than the one before.
>
> Answer 4, 7, 10, 13, 16, 19

Number sequences in co-ordinates

> What patterns can you see in these co-ordinates? (6,4) (8,3) (10,2)
>
> Describe the pattern in the first numbers of each pair (the *x* **co-ordinates**).
>
> Then describe the pattern in the second numbers (the *y* co-ordinates).
>
> Answer The *x* co-ordinate increases by 2 each time.
> The *y* co-ordinate decreases by 1 each time.

Test yourself

1. Fill in the missing numbers.
   a 2 ___ ___ ___ 22
   b 3 ___ ___ ___ 35
   c 24 ___ ___ ___ 0
   d 1 ___ ___ ___ 21
   e 36 ___ ___ ___ 8

2. Fill in the missing numbers. You may need to use negative numbers.
   a 8 ___ ___ ___ ___ –2
   b –3 ___ ___ ___ ___ 17
   c 21 ___ ___ ___ –19
   d –3 ___ ___ ___ ___ –23
   e 32 ___ ___ –4

Remember

When filling in numbers missing from a sequence:

- find the difference
- count the gaps
- divide the difference by the number of gaps.

More number sequences

Multiplication sequences

Multiplication **sequences** change because the number is multiplied each time.

1	2	4	8	16	32	64...	← ×2
3	9	27	81	243...			← ×3
0.0345	3.45	345...					← ×100

Division sequences

Division sequences change because the number is divided each time.

288	144	72	36	18...	← ÷2
25 000	5000	1000	200	40...	← ÷5
760 000	76 000	7600...			← ÷10

Make sure you know how to multiply or divide a number by 10, 100 or 1000. If you are unsure, look at the information on pages 42 and 43.

Fraction sequences

Fraction sequences change because either the **denominator** (bottom number), **numerator** (top number) or both are changing.

They can also involve **mixed numbers** or **improper fractions** (see page 19 for more information on these).

$\frac{1}{2}$ $\frac{1}{3}$ $\frac{1}{4}$ $\frac{1}{5}$ $\frac{1}{6}$ ← the denominator has changed. It is going up by 1 each time.

$\frac{1}{6}$ $\frac{2}{6}$ $\frac{3}{6}$ $\frac{4}{6}$ $\frac{5}{6}$ ← the numerator has changed. It is going up by 1 each time.

$\frac{1}{4}$ $\frac{3}{8}$ $\frac{1}{2}$ $\frac{5}{8}$ $\frac{3}{4}$ ← both the numerator and the denominator have changed. The fractions are going up by $\frac{1}{8}$ each time.

Test yourself

1. Continue and explain these patterns.
   a 350   3500   35 000 ___ ___ ___
   b 4   24   144   864 ___ ___ ___

2. Continue and explain these patterns.
   a 96   48   24   12 ___ ___ ___
   b 246   2.46   0.0246 ___ ___ ___
   c $\frac{2}{9}$ $\frac{3}{9}$ $\frac{4}{9}$ $\frac{5}{9}$ $\frac{6}{9}$ ___ ___ ___

3. Multiply each of these numbers by 10, then by 100, then by 1000.
   a 5   b 64   c 87   d 238   e 534   f 697

4. Divide each of these numbers by 10, then by 100, then by 1000.
   a 6000   b 7200   c 69 000   d 1264   e 6503   f 11 001

Remember

Always check that the rule works between each number in the sequence.

Following rules

Sometimes you may be asked to continue a number sequence by following a rule, as in the examples below.

The rule is 'Double the last number and add 1'. Write the next two numbers in the sequence.

1   3   7   15   —   —

| Double and add 1 | Double and add 1 | Double and add 1 | Double and add 1 | Double and add 1 |

15 ⟶ double and add 1 ⟶ 31 ⟶ double and add 1 ⟶ 63

Answer The next two numbers in the sequence are: 31 63

The rule is 'Double the last number and subtract 1'. Write the next two numbers in the sequence.

8   15   29   57   —   —

| Double and subtract 1 | Double and subtract 1 | Double and subtract 1 | Double and subtract 1 | Double and subtract 1 |

57 ⟶ double and subtract 1 ⟶ 113 ⟶ double and subtract 1 ⟶ 225

Answer The next two numbers in the sequence are: 113 225

The first two numbers are 3.1 and 3.2. The third number is 6.3.
The rule is 'To get the next number, add the two previous numbers'.
Write the next two numbers in the sequence.

3.1   3.2   6.3   —   —

| Add the two previous numbers | Add the two previous numbers | Add the two previous numbers | Add the two previous numbers |

3.1 + 3.2 = 6.3 ⟶ 3.2 + 6.3 = 9.5 ⟶ 6.3 + 9.5 = 15.8

Answer The sequence continues: 9.5 15.8

Test yourself

1. Write the missing numbers in these sequences.
    a The rule is 'Double the last number and add 4'
       5 14 32 ___ ___
    b The rule is 'Halve the last number and add 10'
       4 12 16 ___ ___
    c The rule is 'Multiply the last number by 2 and then add 1'
       6 13 27 ___ ___

Remember

Read the rules for the sequences carefully before you begin.

Roman numerals

The Romans used a number system that didn't include zero. All the numbers from 1 to 100 are written using five letters: I, V, X, L, C.

$I = 1$ $V = 5$ $X = 10$ $L = 50$ $C = 100$

There are rules as to how you can use the letters.

A letter can be repeated to show itself two or three times. However, VV or LL are not used because there is another letter for 10 (X) and one for 100 (C).

$XXX = 30$

$CC = 200$

If one or more letters are placed after another letter of greater value, add that amount.

$VI = 6 (5 + 1 = 6)$

$LXX = 70 (50 + 10 + 10 = 70)$

If I or X is placed before another letter of greater value, subtract that amount.

$IV = 4 (5 - 1 = 4)$

$XC = 90 (100 - 10 = 90)$

For numbers above 100, two more letters are used. Similar rules apply to these letters.

$D = 500$ $M = 1000$

1	I	14	XIV	27	XXVII	150	CL
2	II	15	XV	28	XXVIII	200	CC
3	III	16	XVI	29	XXIX	300	CCC
4	IV	17	XVII	30	XXX	400	CD
5	V	18	XVIII	31	XXXI	500	D
6	VI	19	XIX	40	XL	600	DC
7	VII	20	XX	50	L	700	DCC
8	VIII	21	XXI	60	LX	800	DCCC
9	IX	22	XXII	70	LXX	900	CM
10	X	23	XXIII	80	LXXX	1000	M
11	XI	24	XXIV	90	XC	1600	MDC
12	XII	25	XXV	100	C	1700	MDCC
13	XIII	26	XXVI	101	CI	1900	MCM

Test yourself

1. Which of these years does MLXVII show?
   1947   2014   1067   1017

2. Write these using Roman numerals.
   a 47   **b** 593   **c** 1005   **d** 2144

3. Write each of these Roman numerals as numbers.
   a LXXVI   **b** CCXXVIII   **c** MCMLXI

Remember

No more than three of the same letter can be used. You cannot write XXXX for 40. You must use L and put an X in front to show ten less than 50 (XL).

Fractions

A fraction is part of something that has been split into equal parts. Fractions are written using two numbers, one on top of the other.

The top number, or **numerator**, shows how many of the equal parts we are talking about.

$$\frac{3}{8}$$

The bottom number, or **denominator**, shows how many equal parts the whole has been split into.

Comparing fractions

You can use a fraction wall like the one below to help you compare the sizes of fractions.

Each horizontal strip is one whole, so $\frac{1}{2}$ is worth the same as $\frac{2}{4}$.

one whole										
$\frac{1}{2}$						$\frac{1}{2}$				
$\frac{1}{3}$				$\frac{1}{3}$				$\frac{1}{3}$		
$\frac{1}{4}$			$\frac{1}{4}$			$\frac{1}{4}$			$\frac{1}{4}$		
$\frac{1}{5}$		$\frac{1}{5}$		$\frac{1}{5}$		$\frac{1}{5}$		$\frac{1}{5}$	
$\frac{1}{6}$	$\frac{1}{6}$	$\frac{1}{6}$		$\frac{1}{6}$	$\frac{1}{6}$		$\frac{1}{6}$		
$\frac{1}{8}$	$\frac{1}{8}$	$\frac{1}{8}$	$\frac{1}{8}$	$\frac{1}{8}$	$\frac{1}{8}$	$\frac{1}{8}$	$\frac{1}{8}$		
$\frac{1}{10}$	$\frac{1}{10}$	$\frac{1}{10}$	$\frac{1}{10}$	$\frac{1}{10}$	$\frac{1}{10}$	$\frac{1}{10}$	$\frac{1}{10}$	$\frac{1}{10}$	$\frac{1}{10}$

Another easy way to compare fractions is to make sure both fractions have the same denominator, for example, $\frac{3}{7}$ and $\frac{5}{7}$.

Test yourself

1. What fractions of these shapes are shaded?

a 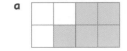 b   c

2. Use the fraction wall to compare these fractions. Which is larger:

a $\frac{1}{2}$ or $\frac{1}{3}$ c $\frac{1}{4}$ or $\frac{2}{10}$ e $\frac{5}{8}$ or $\frac{7}{10}$

b $\frac{1}{3}$ or $\frac{2}{5}$ d $\frac{2}{3}$ or $\frac{5}{8}$ f $\frac{3}{4}$ or $\frac{4}{6}$?

Remember

If you make sure both fractions have the same denominator, it is easier to compare them.

Equivalent fractions

Equivalent fractions stand for the same amount. They can look very different but are worth the same. Here are some equivalent fractions.

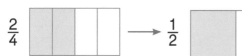

If you can multiply or divide the **numerator** and the **denominator** by the same number, then both fractions are equivalent.

$$\frac{2}{3} \xrightarrow{\times 2} \frac{4}{6} \quad (\times 2)$$

$$\frac{12}{15} \xrightarrow{\div 3} \frac{4}{5} \quad (\div 3)$$

Finding an equivalent fraction

To find an equivalent fraction you can multiply or divide the numerator and the denominator of a fraction by any number you choose. The new fraction will be equivalent.

$$\frac{1}{6} \xrightarrow{\times 5} \frac{5}{30} \quad (\times 5)$$

$$\frac{20}{24} \xrightarrow{\div 4} \frac{5}{6} \quad (\div 4)$$

$$\frac{300}{500} \xrightarrow{\div 100} \frac{3}{5} \quad (\div 100)$$

Cancelling a fraction to its simplest (or lowest) form

When you divide the numerator and the denominator by the largest number you can, and can't divide again by any other number, you have cancelled the fraction to its simplest (or lowest) form.

> Cancel these fractions to their simplest form
>
> $$\frac{4}{28} \xrightarrow{\div 4} \frac{1}{7} \quad (\div 4)$$
>
> $$\frac{50}{70} \xrightarrow{\div 10} \frac{5}{7} \quad (\div 10)$$
>
> $$\frac{30}{51} \xrightarrow{\div 3} \frac{10}{17} \quad (\div 3)$$

You might be asked to give some fractions that are equivalent to another fraction, like this.

> Give three fractions equivalent to $\frac{3}{5}$
>
> $$\frac{3}{5} \xrightarrow{\times 2} \frac{6}{10} \quad (\times 2)$$
>
> $$\frac{3}{5} \xrightarrow{\times 3} \frac{9}{15} \quad (\times 3)$$
>
> $$\frac{3}{5} \xrightarrow{\times 10} \frac{30}{50} \quad (\times 10)$$

$$\frac{12}{15} \qquad \frac{4}{5}$$

Remember

If you can multiply the numerator and the denominator by the same number to make another fraction, then both fractions are equivalent.

Test yourself

1. Which of these pairs of fractions are equivalent?

   a $\frac{3}{5}$ and $\frac{9}{15}$

   b $\frac{3}{5}$ and $\frac{12}{16}$

   c $\frac{3}{8}$ and $\frac{9}{24}$

   d $\frac{15}{18}$ and $\frac{5}{6}$

   e $\frac{12}{20}$ and $\frac{3}{5}$

2. Cancel these fractions to their simplest form.

   a $\frac{6}{24}$ c $\frac{8}{22}$

   b $\frac{15}{18}$ d $\frac{20}{28}$

3. Give three fractions equivalent to:

   a $\frac{3}{4}$ c $\frac{100}{500}$

   b $\frac{30}{40}$ d $\frac{2}{3}$

Schofield & Sims

Mixed numbers and improper fractions

Mixed numbers

This is a **mixed number**:

$$4\frac{1}{2}$$

A mixed number contains a whole number (4) and a fraction ($\frac{1}{2}$).

Improper fractions

An **improper fraction** is sometimes called a 'top-heavy' fraction because the numerator (top number) is larger than the denominator. Improper fractions are worth more than one whole. These are improper fractions:

$$\frac{5}{2} \quad \frac{7}{3} \quad \frac{9}{6} \quad \frac{10}{2}$$

Change $5\frac{3}{4}$ to an improper fraction

There are four quarters in a whole one. There are five whole ones, so that's 20 quarters. Add on the other three quarters.

That makes $\frac{23}{4}$.

$5\frac{3}{4}$ is $\frac{23}{4}$

A quick way of working this out is to say, '4 times 5 equals 20, add 3, equals 23'.

Answer $\frac{23}{4}$

Change $\frac{23}{4}$ to a mixed number

There are four quarters in a whole one. There are 23 quarters, so that's five whole ones, and three quarters left over.

That makes $5\frac{3}{4}$.

$\frac{23}{4}$ is $5\frac{3}{4}$

A quick way of working this out is to say, '23 divided by 4 is 5 and 3 left over'.

Answer $5\frac{3}{4}$

Test yourself

1. Change these mixed numbers to improper fractions.

   a $3\frac{1}{2}$ **c** $2\frac{1}{4}$ **e** $5\frac{1}{3}$ **g** $6\frac{3}{5}$

   b $5\frac{1}{2}$ **d** $4\frac{3}{4}$ **f** $7\frac{2}{3}$ **h** $5\frac{2}{5}$

2. Change these improper fractions to mixed numbers.

   a $\frac{8}{3}$ **c** $\frac{15}{2}$ **e** $\frac{16}{5}$ **g** $\frac{22}{5}$

   b $\frac{9}{4}$ **d** $\frac{21}{4}$ **f** $\frac{18}{8}$ **h** $\frac{37}{10}$

Remember

Mixed numbers contain a whole number and a fraction.

Improper fractions are top heavy. They have a numerator larger than the denominator.

Ordering fractions

When ordering fractions it is a good idea to **convert** them all so that they all have the same **denominator** (bottom number).

Order these fractions in ascending order.

$$\frac{1}{2} \quad \frac{5}{8} \quad \frac{3}{4} \quad \frac{3}{16}$$

Which number do all the denominators go into? 16

$$\frac{1}{2} \xrightarrow{\times 8} \frac{8}{16} \qquad \frac{3}{4} \xrightarrow{\times 4} \frac{12}{16}$$

$$\frac{5}{8} \xrightarrow{\times 2} \frac{10}{16} \qquad \frac{3}{16} \xrightarrow{} \frac{3}{16}$$

Now they all have the same denominator you can order them. In this case, in ascending order (smallest to largest).

$$\frac{3}{16} \quad \frac{8}{16} \quad \frac{10}{16} \quad \frac{12}{16}$$

Remember to write them in their original state rather than the one you have converted them into.

Answer $\frac{3}{16} \quad \frac{1}{2} \quad \frac{5}{8} \quad \frac{3}{4}$

If ordering **mixed numbers**, look at the whole numbers first as it may reduce the number of fractions you need to convert.

Order these fractions in descending order.

$$1\frac{2}{3} \quad 2\frac{1}{5} \quad 1\frac{5}{6} \quad \frac{3}{7}$$

$2\frac{1}{5}$ is clearly the largest fraction as it has the largest whole number.

$\frac{3}{7}$ is clearly the smallest fraction as it is not a mixed number.

That means you only need to compare $1\frac{2}{3}$ and $1\frac{5}{6}$ to find out which is bigger.

Both denominators will go into 6.

$$\frac{2}{3} \xrightarrow{\times 2} \frac{4}{6} \quad \text{so } 1\frac{2}{3} = 1\frac{4}{6}$$

$$\frac{5}{6} \xrightarrow{=} \frac{5}{6} \quad \text{so } 1\frac{5}{6} = 1\frac{5}{6}$$

Now you can order them. This time in descending order (largest to smallest).

$$2\frac{1}{5} \quad 1\frac{5}{6} \quad 1\frac{4}{6} \quad \frac{3}{7}$$

Remember to write them in their original state rather than the one you have converted them into.

Answer $2\frac{1}{5} \quad 1\frac{5}{6} \quad 1\frac{2}{3} \quad \frac{3}{7}$

Remember

When writing fractions in order, always write them in their original state rather than the one you have converted them into.

Test yourself

1. Order these fractions in ascending order.

   a $\frac{2}{5} \quad \frac{3}{10} \quad \frac{1}{2} \quad \frac{17}{20}$

   b $1\frac{1}{4} \quad 2\frac{2}{7} \quad \frac{3}{10} \quad 1\frac{7}{16}$

2. Order these fractions in descending order.

   a $\frac{3}{6} \quad \frac{1}{4} \quad \frac{5}{8} \quad \frac{11}{12}$

   b $5\frac{1}{3} \quad 2\frac{7}{9} \quad 2\frac{1}{3} \quad 4\frac{5}{6}$

Finding fractions

Find fractions of an amount in your head

Fractions with a **numerator** (top number) of 1 are called unit fractions. These are unit fractions:

$$\frac{1}{2} \quad \frac{1}{5} \quad \frac{1}{6} \quad \frac{1}{10}$$

Find a unit fraction of a number

Divide the number by the **denominator**.

$\frac{1}{5}$ of 45 $\longrightarrow$ 45 ÷ 5 = 9 $\qquad$ $\frac{1}{8}$ of 56 $\longrightarrow$ 56 ÷ 8 = 7

Find any fraction of a number

Find the unit fraction first, then multiply.

$\frac{1}{5}$ of 45 $\longrightarrow$ 45 ÷ 5 = 9 $\qquad$ So $\frac{2}{5}$ of 45 = 9 × 2 = 18

one-fifth $\quad$ two-fifths

$\frac{1}{8}$ of 56 $\longrightarrow$ 56 ÷ 8 = 7 $\qquad$ So $\frac{5}{8}$ of 56 = 7 × 5 = 35

one-eighth $\quad$ five-eighths

Find fractions with a calculator

You can find fractions using a calculator. Divide by the denominator (unit fraction) and then multiply by the numerator, as before.

To check whether you divided and multiplied correctly, see if your answer looks 'about right'.

> Find $\frac{5}{9}$ of £108
>
> Key in **1 0 8 ÷ 9 × 5** which gives 60.
>
> Answer **60**
>
> Check: $\frac{5}{9}$ is a bit more than $\frac{1}{2}$, so $\frac{5}{9}$ of £108 should be a bit more than half of £108. £60 is about right. If you had got it the wrong way round, the answer would have been larger than £108.

Test yourself

1. Find these unit fractions.

   a $\frac{1}{4}$ of 24 $\qquad$ b $\frac{1}{3}$ of 18 $\qquad$ c $\frac{1}{7}$ of 42 $\qquad$ d $\frac{1}{8}$ of 32

2. Find these fractions without using a calculator.

   a $\frac{3}{4}$ of 32 $\qquad$ b $\frac{3}{5}$ of 40 $\qquad$ c $\frac{5}{6}$ of £48 $\qquad$ d $\frac{5}{8}$ of 48 kg

3. Use a calculator to find these fractions.

   a $\frac{4}{7}$ of 56 $\qquad$ b $\frac{3}{5}$ of 105 kg $\qquad$ c $\frac{7}{9}$ of 135 cm $\qquad$ d $\frac{6}{7}$ of £91

Remember

To find unit fractions: divide by the denominator.

To find other fractions: find the unit fraction and then multiply by the numerator.

Adding and subtracting fractions

When adding and subtracting fractions, make sure the fractions have the same denominator (bottom number). Then just add or subtract the numerators (top numbers) and write the same denominator.

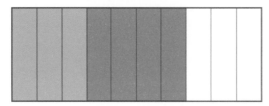

$\frac{3}{10} + \frac{4}{10} = \frac{7}{10}$ ←—— *three-tenths add four-tenths is seven-tenths*

$\frac{11}{12} - \frac{7}{12} = \frac{4}{12}$ ←—— *eleven-twelfths subtract seven-twelfths is four-twelfths*

The answer you get might need to be simplified. If the answer is an improper (top heavy) fraction, it can be changed to a **mixed number**.

$\frac{11}{12} - \frac{7}{12} = \frac{4}{12}$ can be simplified to $\frac{1}{3}$

$\frac{4}{5} + \frac{4}{5} = \frac{8}{5}$ can be changed to the mixed number $1\frac{3}{5}$

If the fractions do not have the same denominator, you need to change one or both of them to **equivalent fractions**.

$\frac{3}{10} + \frac{4}{5} = \frac{3}{10} + \frac{8}{10} = \frac{11}{10} = 1\frac{1}{10}$

Adding and subtracting mixed numbers

You need to add or subtract the whole number part of the second number first.

$4\frac{3}{7} + 2\frac{2}{7} = 4\frac{3}{7} + 2 + \frac{2}{7} = 6\frac{3}{7} + \frac{2}{7} = 6\frac{5}{7}$

With mixed number subtractions, take care if the second fraction is larger than the first.

$5\frac{2}{7} - 1\frac{4}{7} = 5\frac{2}{7} - 1 - \frac{4}{7} = 4\frac{2}{7} - \frac{4}{7} = 3\frac{5}{7}$

Test yourself

Answer these, giving answers as simplified proper fractions or mixed numbers.

1. a $\frac{4}{9} + \frac{1}{9} =$ b $\frac{9}{10} - \frac{2}{10} =$ c $\frac{5}{12} + \frac{1}{12} =$ d $\frac{7}{8} - \frac{5}{8} =$

2. a $\frac{9}{10} - \frac{4}{5} =$ b $\frac{3}{4} - \frac{3}{8} =$ c $\frac{11}{12} - \frac{2}{3} =$ d $\frac{3}{4} - \frac{1}{5} =$

3. a $2\frac{5}{6} - 2\frac{1}{6} =$ b $5\frac{2}{5} - 1\frac{3}{5} =$ c $7\frac{3}{4} + 1\frac{2}{3} =$ d $8\frac{3}{7} - 5\frac{4}{7} =$

Remember

Make sure the fractions have the same denominator before you begin. You only need to add or subtract the numerator.

Multiplying and dividing with fractions

Multiplying fractions

When you multiply a fraction by a whole number, just multiply the **numerator** by the number and write the same **denominator**. Then write the fraction in its simplest form. Change the fraction to a **mixed number**, if asked.

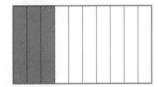

$$\frac{3}{10} \times 4 = \frac{12}{10} = \frac{6}{5} = 1\frac{1}{5}$$

When you multiply two fractions, just multiply the numerators together and the denominators together. Simplify if you can.

$$\frac{3}{10} \times \frac{3}{10} = \frac{9}{100}$$

If you can divide a numerator and a denominator by the same number before multiplying, it can make the calculation easier. The answer in its simplest form will be the same.

$$\frac{8}{9} \times \frac{3}{4} = \frac{24}{36} = \frac{2}{3} \quad \text{or} \quad \frac{8^2}{9_1} \times \frac{3}{4_1} {}_3\!\!= \frac{2}{9} \times \frac{3^1}{1} = \frac{2}{3} \times \frac{1}{1} = \frac{2}{3}$$

Dividing fractions by whole numbers

When you divide a fraction by a whole number, just multiply the denominator by the whole number and write the same numerator. Make sure the fraction is in its simplest form. Change it to a mixed number, if asked.

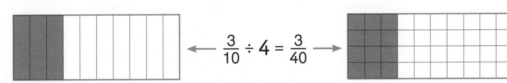

$$\longleftarrow \quad \frac{3}{10} \div 4 = \frac{3}{40} \quad \longrightarrow$$

Multiplying mixed numbers by whole numbers

When multiplying mixed numbers by whole numbers, it is much easier to multiply the whole numbers first and then the fraction.

$$2\frac{2}{3} \times 4 \qquad 2 \times 4 = 8 \qquad \frac{2}{3} \times 4 = \frac{8}{3} \ \left(\frac{8}{3} = 2\frac{2}{3}\right) \qquad 8 + \frac{8}{3} = 10\frac{2}{3}$$

Test yourself

Give your answers as simplified proper fractions or mixed numbers.

1. a $\frac{7}{9} \times 6 =$ **b** $\frac{5}{6} \times 3 =$ **c** $\frac{3}{10} \times 8 =$ **d** $\frac{5}{12} \times 5 =$

2. a $\frac{2}{3} \times \frac{1}{4} =$ **b** $\frac{4}{5} \times \frac{10}{12} =$ **c** $\frac{7}{8} \times \frac{4}{9} =$ **d** $\frac{8}{9} \times \frac{3}{10} =$

3. a $\frac{4}{5} \div 5 =$ **b** $\frac{3}{9} \div 2 =$ **c** $\frac{7}{8} \div 3 =$ **d** $\frac{4}{7} \div 4 =$

Remember

Always simplify your answer and give it in the form asked for in the question.

Decimals

Decimals, like fractions, contain part numbers. You need to know what each digit in a decimal stands for.

    0.1   3.54   102.629

The dot that separates the whole numbers from the part numbers is called the **decimal point**.

    5.96

To the left of the decimal point are the whole numbers. To the right of the decimal point are the tenths, hundredths and thousandths.

tenths   hundredths thousandths

T O . t h th

7 2 . 5 4 9

whole numbers   part numbers

A tenth, or 0.1, is the same as the fraction $\frac{1}{10}$.

A hundredth, or 0.01, is the same as $\frac{1}{100}$.

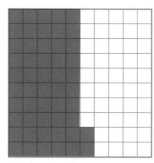

So 0.52 means 5 tenths and 2 hundredths, $\frac{52}{100}$ or 52 hundredths.

Change 0.37 to a fraction

0.37 means 3 tenths and 7 hundredths or 37 hundredths. Write 37 hundredths as a fraction.

Answer $\frac{37}{100}$

Change $\frac{63}{100}$ to a decimal

$\frac{63}{100}$ (63 hundredths) is the same as 0.63.

Answer 0.63

Test yourself

1. Write these decimals as fractions.

    a 0.3 **b** 0.9 **c** 0.54 **d** 0.78 **e** 0.391 **f** 0.004

2. Write these fractions as decimals.

    a $\frac{2}{10}$ **b** $\frac{8}{10}$ **c** $\frac{40}{100}$ **d** $\frac{78}{100}$ **e** $\frac{400}{1000}$ **f** $\frac{301}{1000}$

Remember

0.1   = 1 tenth   = $\frac{1}{10}$

0.01   = 1 hundredth = $\frac{1}{100}$

0.001 = 1 thousandth = $\frac{1}{1000}$

Ordering decimals

Ordering decimals is like ordering whole numbers (see page 8). First, compare the left-hand digits. If they are the same, move one step to the right to compare the next digits, and so on.

Put these decimals in order of size, largest first: 0.783   0.88   0.78   0.9   0.792

Which number has most tenths? ————————————————→ 0.9

Which has the next greatest numbers of tenths? ———————→ 0.88

Which numbers have the next greatest number of tenths? 0.783   0.78   0.792

Which of these has most hundredths? ——————————————→ 0.792

Which numbers have the next greatest number of hundredths? 0.783   0.78

Which of these has more thousandths? ——————————————→ 0.783

Which is the smallest number? ———————————————————→ 0.78

Answer 0.9   0.88   0.792   0.783   0.78

Adding zeros

Some people find it helpful to put extra zeros on the end of the decimals so that each decimal has the same number of digits:

0.783   0.880   0.780   0.900   0.792

This doesn't change the numbers (because 0.9 = 0.90 = 0.900), but it does make them easier to compare, for example:

0.900 is larger than 0.783

By adding the extra zeros, you can see that the correct order is:

0.900   0.880   0.792   0.783   0.780

Test yourself

1. Which is the larger decimal in each pair?
   a 0.8, 0.79
   b 0.37, 0.34
   c 3.658, 3.7

2. Put these decimals in order of size, smallest first.
   a 0.5, 0.8, 0.7, 0.75, 0.62
   b 3.524, 3.56, 3.52, 3.563
   c 0.876, 0.867, 0.687, 0.678

Remember

To order decimals, work from left to right to compare the digits. Putting zeros on the end of a decimal doesn't change its value.

Rounding decimals

Decimals on a number line

Decimals lie between whole numbers.

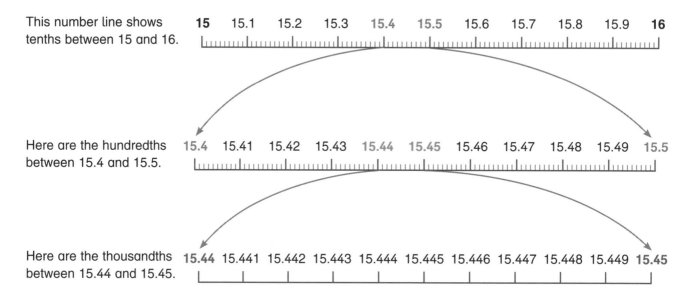

This number line shows tenths between 15 and 16.

Here are the hundredths between 15.4 and 15.5.

Here are the thousandths between 15.44 and 15.45.

Rounding with a number line

You round decimals in exactly the same way as whole numbers (see page 6). This time though, numbers are rounded to the nearest whole number, tenth, hundredth or thousandth, and so on.

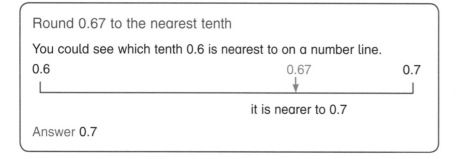

Round 0.67 to the nearest tenth

You could see which tenth 0.6 is nearest to on a number line.

0.6   0.67   0.7

it is nearer to 0.7

Answer **0.7**

see page 6

Remember

Round decimals the same way as for whole numbers.

When rounding 'to the nearest tenth', find the tenths digit and look at the digit to its right.
- If it is 5 or above, the tenths digit goes up one.
- If it is 4 or below, the tenths digit stays the same.

Rounding without a number line

Alternatively, you could do the following.

1. Find out what you are rounding to (here, it is to the nearest tenth).

2. Point to this digit in the number.

3. Look at the digit to the right of it. If it's smaller than 5, the tenths stays the same. If it's 5 or larger, the tenths digit goes up one.

4. 7 is larger than 5 so the answer is 0.7

```
O . t h
0 . 6 7

0 . 6 7

0 . 7
```

Rounding to the nearest tenth may also be referred to as rounding to one decimal place, rounding to the nearest hundredth may also be referred to as rounding to two decimal places and rounding to the nearest thousandth may also be referred to as rounding to three decimal places.

Test yourself

1. Draw a number line with 10 intervals. Show the decimals between 12 and 13.

2. Draw a number line with 10 intervals. Show the decimals between 8.5 and 8.6.

3. Round these numbers to one decimal place.
   a 0.84   d 0.85
   b 0.37   e 0.492
   c 4.56   f 0.549

Percentages

Percentages can also be used to show parts of a whole. A **percentage** is a fraction with a **denominator** of 100, but written in a different way.

$$36\% \longrightarrow \frac{36}{100}$$

Per cent means 'out of a hundred'. Thirty-six per cent is '36 out of 100'.

These percentages, fractions and decimals have the same value.

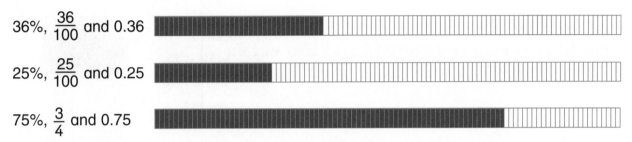

36%, $\frac{36}{100}$ and 0.36

25%, $\frac{25}{100}$ and 0.25

75%, $\frac{3}{4}$ and 0.75

You can place them all on a number line, as in the example below.

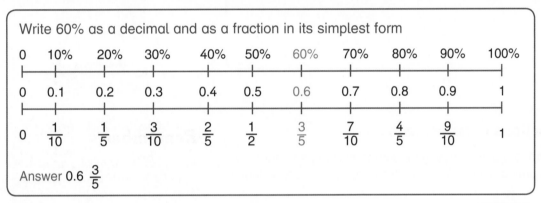

Write 60% as a decimal and as a fraction in its simplest form

0	10%	20%	30%	40%	50%	60%	70%	80%	90%	100%

0	0.1	0.2	0.3	0.4	0.5	0.6	0.7	0.8	0.9	1

0	$\frac{1}{10}$	$\frac{1}{5}$	$\frac{3}{10}$	$\frac{2}{5}$	$\frac{1}{2}$	$\frac{3}{5}$	$\frac{7}{10}$	$\frac{4}{5}$	$\frac{9}{10}$	1

Answer 0.6 $\frac{3}{5}$

Converting percentages to decimals

You **convert** a percentage to a decimal by dividing by 100.

$36\% \longrightarrow 36 \div 100 = 0.36$

$75\% \longrightarrow 75 \div 100 = 0.75$

$64\% \longrightarrow 64 \div 100 = 0.64$

Converting decimals to percentages

You convert a decimal to a percentage by multiplying by 100.

$0.7 \longrightarrow 0.7 \times 100 = 70\%$

$0.38 \longrightarrow 0.38 \times 100 = 38\%$

$0.11 \longrightarrow 0.11 \times 100 = 11\%$

Test yourself

1. Write these percentages as decimals.
   a 25%   c 34%   e 90%
   b 50%   d 89%   f 73%

2. Write these percentages as fractions in their simplest form.
   a 28%   c 48%   e 19%
   b 72%   d 80%   f 99%

Converting percentages to fractions

First, you write the percentage as a fraction with a denominator of 100.

Then find the simplest form by dividing the **numerator** and denominator by the same number.

> Convert 36% to a fraction
>
> Begin by writing the percentage as a fraction with a denominator of 100.
>
> $36\% = \dfrac{36}{100}$
>
> Now divide the numerator and denominator by the same number to find the simplest form.
>
>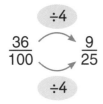
>
> Answer $\dfrac{9}{25}$

Converting fractions to percentages

To convert a fraction to a percentage, you need to multiply both the numerator and denominator by a number which will make a denominator of 100.

> Change $\frac{11}{20}$ into a fraction with a denominator of 100
>
> Multiply by ×5, as 20 × 5 = 100.
>
> $\dfrac{11}{20} \quad \xrightarrow{\times 5} \quad \dfrac{?}{100} = \dfrac{55}{100}$ (this is the same as 55%)
>
> Answer 55%

If the denominator of the fraction is not a **factor** of 100, for example $\frac{3}{8}$, divide the numerator by the denominator to find the decimal.

$$3 \div 8 = 0.375$$

Then multiply it by 100.

$$0.375 \times 100 = 37.5 \longrightarrow 37.5\%$$

Remember

Always think of the % sign as 'out of 100' or 'divided by 100'. A percentage is a fraction with a denominator of 100.

Test yourself

1. Write these percentages as fractions in their simplest form.
   a 27%
   b 52%
   c 87%

2. Write these fractions as percentages.
   a $\frac{3}{5}$
   b $\frac{7}{10}$
   c $\frac{6}{20}$

3. Find these percentages.
   a 50% of £72
   b 50% of 48m
   c 25% of £600
   d 25% of 120kg
   e 75% of 680cm

Finding percentages

Finding percentages in your head

There are several ways to find a **percentage** of a number or amount in your head.

- To find 50%: halve the number
  50% of £480 ⟶ half of £480 = £240

- To find 25%: halve the number and halve again (or just divide by 4)
  25% of £480 ⟶ half of £480 = £240, half of £240 = £120

- To find 75%: halve the number and halve again, then add the two answers
  75% of £480 ⟶ half of £480 = £240, half of £240 = £120, £240 + £120 = £360

Finding other percentages in your head

To find other percentages in your head, you can use this scale divided into 10% sections:

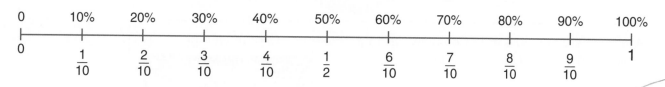

- To find 10%: divide the number by 10
  10% of 800 ⟶ 800 ÷ 10 ⟶ 80
  10% of £480 ⟶ £480 ÷ 10 ⟶ £48

- To find 20%: divide by 10 and double
  20% of 800 ⟶ 800 ÷ 10 = 80 ⟶ 80 × 2 = 160
  20% of £480 ⟶ £480 ÷ 10 = £48 ⟶ £48 × 2 = £96

- To find 30%: divide by 10 and multiply by 3
  30% of 800 ⟶ 800 ÷ 10 = 80 ⟶ 80 × 3 = 240

- To find 40%: divide by 10 and multiply by 4, and so on.
  40% of £480 ⟶ £480 ÷ 10 = £48 ⟶ £48 × 4 = £192

Test yourself

1. Find 10% of these amounts.
   a £120
   b 450kg
   c 254km

2. Find 30% of these amounts.
   a £250
   b 400kg
   c 160cm

3. Find 70% of these amounts.
   a £80
   b 90kg
   c 250m

4. I have £260 in my bank account. I earn 5% interest on this money. How much interest do I earn?

Remember

For all percentages that are multiples of 10, use your answer to 10% to help you.

Percentage problems

Solving percentage problems

You can use these skills to help you solve percentage problems.

In a sale, you pay 60% of the normal price. The normal price for this is £40. How much is the sale price?

To find 60% of £40, find 10% of £40 (£4) and then multiply by 6

Answer £24

A woman spends 30% of her earnings on rent. She earns £24 000 in a year. How much does she spend on rent?

To find 30% of £24 000, find 10% of £24 000 (£2400) and then multiply by 3

Answer £7200

A school trip of 40 children go to a museum. 75% of the children take a packed lunch. How many children do not?

First find the percentage of children who do not take a packed lunch.
100% − 75% = 25%

To find 25% of 40, find 10% of 40 (4) then multiply by 2.5

Answer 10

Test yourself

1. A bottle holds 250ml of orange juice. If Henry drinks 40% of the juice, how much does he drink?

2. There are 80 children in the park. 30% of them are boys. How many are boys?

3. 95% of passengers on a bus will get off before the end. If there are 60 passengers, how many will still be on the bus at the end?

Remember

To solve percentage problems, first find easy percentages and use them to find others.

Fractions, decimals and percentages

Fractions, decimals and percentages are different ways of saying the same thing. This diagram shows how to change between them.

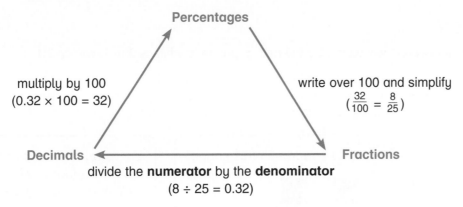

Percentages

multiply by 100
(0.32 × 100 = 32)

write over 100 and simplify
($\frac{32}{100} = \frac{8}{25}$)

Decimals **Fractions**

divide the **numerator** by the **denominator**
(8 ÷ 25 = 0.32)

When solving percentage problems, it can sometimes be easier to change the percentage to a fraction or decimal.

Jack has £175 and has to pay 32% in tax. How much tax has he to pay?

Change 32% to a fraction and simplify it:

$$\frac{32}{100} = \frac{8}{25} \text{ so } \frac{8}{25} \text{ of } 175 = 175 \div 25 \times 8$$
$$= 7 \times 8 = £56$$

Answer £56

Erin has £56 in a bank account. The bank gives her 8% of this amount in interest. How much interest does she get?

Change 8% to a decimal:

8% of £56 is 0.08 × 56 or 8 × 56 ÷ 100

$$\begin{array}{r} 5\ 6 \\ \times\ \ 8 \\ \hline 4\ 4\ 8 \\ {\scriptstyle 4} \end{array}$$ so 448 ÷ 100 = £4.48

Answer £4.48

Test yourself

1. Use any appropriate method to find:
   a 4% of £225   c 16% of £125   e 45% of £80
   b 7% of £32   d 8% of £175

2. Solve these problems.
   a A puppy weighs 64% of its expected weight. Its expected weight was 95 ounces. How much does it weigh?
   b A train travels at 72mph. It slows down to 45% of that speed. How fast is it travelling now?
   c A garage adds 17.5% VAT to the cost of a repair. How much is the VAT for a repair costing £162?

Remember

It is important to know the relationship between the following fractions, decimals and percentages.

$\frac{1}{2} = 0.5 = 50\%$ $\frac{1}{8} = 0.125 = 12.5\%$

$\frac{1}{4} = 0.25 = 25\%$ $\frac{1}{10} = 0.1 = 10\%$

$\frac{1}{5} = 0.2 = 20\%$ $\frac{1}{25} = 0.04 = 4\%$

Ratio and proportion

You can use **ratio** to compare the purple parts with the white parts of this rectangle.

There are 3 purple parts for every 1 white part. So the ratio of purple to white is 3 to 1, written 3:1.

You can use **proportion** to compare the purple parts with the whole rectangle. 3 in every 4 parts are purple. So the proportion of purple parts is 3 out of 4. Think of proportion as a fraction: the fraction that is purple is $\frac{3}{4}$. You can also write this proportion as 0.75 or 75%.

Use ratio to compare the blue and white squares in this shape

There are 6 blue squares and 3 white squares.

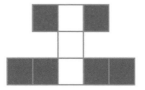

Answer The ratio is 6 to 3 (6:3), simplified to 2:1.

Use proportion to compare the blue squares with the total number of squares

There are 6 blue squares out of a total of 9.

Answer The proportion is 6 out of 9 ($\frac{6}{9}$), simplified to $\frac{2}{3}$.

Scale factor

The **scale factor** is the ratio between two shapes where one has been made bigger or smaller.

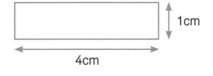

1cm

4cm

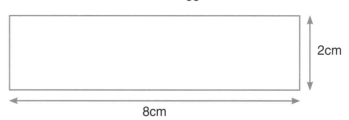

2cm

8cm

The second rectangle has been increased by a scale factor of 2 as both the length and width have been doubled (× 2).

Test yourself

1. Look at the squares in this shape.

   a What proportion of the squares is red?

   b What fraction of the squares is red?

   c What is the ratio of red to white squares?

2. Look at the box of chocolates.

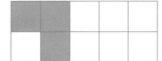

   a What proportion of the chocolates is round?

   b What fraction of the chocolates is round?

   c What is the ratio of round to square chocolates?

3. If a square with sides 4cm is increased by a scale factor of 3, what is the length of the new sides?

Remember

Ratio compares 'part with part' ('for every' or 'to every').

Proportion compares 'part with whole' ('in every' or 'out of every').

Ratio and proportion problems

How many plain chairs to spotty chairs are there below? What fraction of all the chairs are plain?

Answer Plain chairs to spotty chairs (**ratio**): 5:3

The fraction of chairs that are plain (**proportion**): $\frac{5}{8}$

Ben has 4 books for every 1 that Caitlin has. Ben has 12 books. How many has Caitlin?

Write pairs of numbers in the ratio of 4:1.

Ben	Caitlin
4	1
8	2
12	3

Answer Caitlin has 3 books.

Dev makes soup using 3 peppers for every 2 tomatoes. He uses 15 peppers. How many tomatoes does he use?

Write pairs of numbers in the ratio of 3:2.

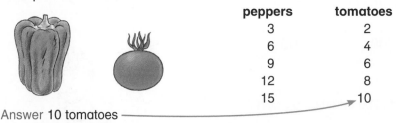

peppers	tomatoes
3	2
6	4
9	6
12	8
15	10

Answer 10 tomatoes

There are 32 pupils in a class in the ratio 3 boys to every 5 girls, or 3:5. How many boys are there?

Find the proportion of boys in the class by adding the numbers in the ratio.

3 boys + 5 girls = 8 pupils. 3 out of 8 pupils are boys ($\frac{3}{8}$).

Find $\frac{3}{8}$ of 32. Find $\frac{1}{8}$ by dividing 32 by 8 $\longrightarrow$ 32 ÷ 8 = 4.

If $\frac{1}{8}$ is 4, then $\frac{3}{8}$ is 4 × 3 = 12.

So 12 out of 32 pupils are boys.

Answer 12

Remember

You can change ratios to their simplest form. For example:

9:6 $\longrightarrow$ 3:2

15:3 $\longrightarrow$ 5:1

12:28 $\longrightarrow$ 3:7

Test yourself

1. Oscar shares out 15 grapes. He gives Sima 1 for every 4 he eats. How many does Sima get?

2. At the tennis club there are 2 boys for every 3 girls. There are 20 children altogether. How many are boys?

3. There are 4 toffees to every 3 chocolates in a bag of 28 sweets. How many toffees are there?

Mental addition and subtraction

Adding and subtracting 10 and 100

To add or subtract 10, add or subtract 'one' from the digit in the tens column.

$$529 + 10 = 539 \qquad 529 - 10 = 519$$

To add or subtract 100, add or subtract 'one' from the digit in the hundreds column.

$$1467 + 100 = 1567 \qquad 1467 - 100 = 1367$$

Adding or subtracting near multiples of 10

A near **multiple** of 10 is a number like 49 or 58. To add or subtract them, add or subtract the multiple of 10 first, and adjust afterwards as shown below.

$$39 + 54 \longrightarrow 40 + 54 = 94 \longrightarrow \text{subtract } 1 \longrightarrow 93$$
$$76 - 48 \longrightarrow 76 - 50 = 26 \longrightarrow \text{add } 2 \longrightarrow 28$$

For near multiples of 100, use the same method to add and subtract numbers, as in the next example. Always check whether you need to adjust by adding or subtracting!

$$574 + 97 \longrightarrow 574 + 100 = 674 \longrightarrow \text{subtract } 3 \longrightarrow 671$$
$$837 - 198 \longrightarrow 837 - 200 = 637 \longrightarrow \text{add } 2 \longrightarrow 639$$

Using blank number lines

When counting on or back through 10, 100, 1000 and so on, use blank number lines.

Find the difference between 705 and 687

Draw a line with 687 at the left end and 705 at the right.

687   700   705

13   5

Write 700 on the line. Count from 687 to 700 and then on to 705.
Add $13 + 5 = 18$.

Answer **18**

$574 + 97 = ?$

Test yourself

1. Add 10 to these numbers.
   a 94   b 392   c 996

2. Subtract 10 from these numbers.
   a 107   b 701   c 1005

3. Add or subtract these numbers.
   a $49 + 26$ b $134 + 58$ c $78 - 49$ d $354 - 151$

4. Find the difference between:
   a 703 and 689   c 1294 and 1307
   b 608 and 591   d 2609 and 2578

Remember

Use these strategies to help you add and subtract numbers in your head.

Written addition

Sometimes numbers get too large to work with in your head, so you need another method. When adding numbers on paper, make sure you line the columns up correctly and approximate first.

---

565 + 234

Approximation: 600 + 200 = 800

	H	T	O
	5	6	5
+	2	3	4
	7	9	9

This calculation has no carrying.

Answer 799

Remember

You need to line up the decimal points, as the decimal point separates whole numbers from 'part numbers'.

7538 + 26 904

Approximation: 8000 + 27 000 = 35 000

	TTh	Th	H	T	O
		7	5	3	8
+	2	6	9	0	4
	3	4	4	4	2
	1	1		1	

This calculation has lots of carrying. Follow the boxes from right to left if you're not sure.

0 + 2 + 1 = 3, write 3 in the ten thousands column	7 + 6 + 1 = 14, write 4 and carry one ten thousand	5 + 9 = 14, write 4 and carry one thousand into the thousands column	3 + 0 + 1 = 4, write 4 in the tens column	8 + 4 = 12, write 2 and carry one ten into the tens column

←

Answer 34 442

Adding decimals

Add decimals in the same way as whole numbers. Just be careful to line up each column and each **decimal point** correctly.

36.3 + 52.86

Approximation: 36 + 53 = 89

	T	O	.	t	h
	3	6	.	3	0	← put a 0 here
+	5	2	.	8	6
	8	9	.	1	6
				1	

Answer 89.16

Test yourself

1. Approximate first, then add these numbers.
   a 431 + 56
   b 658 + 297
   c 1739 + 2047
   d 3917 + 5009

2. Approximate first, then add these decimal numbers.
   a 21.5 + 16.4
   b 36.8 + 27.1
   c 87.19 + 16.8
   d 152.87 + 305.74

Written subtraction

When subtracting large numbers on paper, line the columns up correctly and approximate first. Watch out for when you need to exchange.

647 – 432

Approximation: 600 – 400 = 200

H	T	O
6	4	7
– 4	3	2
2	1	5

Answer 215

This calculation has no exchange.

Check your answer by adding the last two rows:
432 + 215 = 647

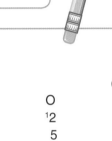

7632 – 2815

Approximation: 8000 – 3000 = 5000

Th	H	T	O
7̶ 6	¹6	3̶ 2	¹2
– 2	8	1	5
4	8	1	7

| 6 – 2 = 4, write 4. | You can't do 6 – 8, so borrow one thousand and change it into 10 hundreds. Cross out one of the thousands. Take 8 from 16. Write 8. | 2 – 1 = 1. Write 1 in the tens column. | You can't do 2 – 5, so borrow one ten and change it into 10 ones. Cross out one of the tens. The 2 becomes 12. Take 5 from 12. Write 7. |

This calculation needs exchanges. Follow the boxes from right to left if you're not sure.

Answer 4817

Subtracting decimals

You can subtract decimals in the same way as whole numbers. Just be careful to line up each column and each decimal point correctly.

52.97 – 36.8

Approximation: 53 – 37 = 16

T	O	.	t	h
5̶ 4	¹2	.	9	7
– 3	6	.	8	0	← put a 0 here
1	6	.	1	7

Answer 16.17

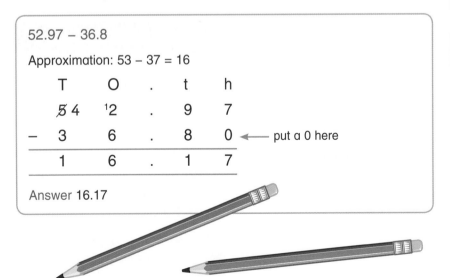

Remember

Be careful to write the numbers correctly on paper and line them up.

Test yourself

1. Approximate first, then subtract these numbers.
   a 685 – 43
   b 548 – 339
   c 2794 – 1697
   d 3408 – 2619

2. Approximate first, then subtract these decimals.
   a 32.5 – 21.4
   b 56.9 – 27.3
   c 76.15 – 38.26
   d 540.31 – 406.54

Factors, multiples and prime numbers

Factors

Factors are whole numbers that divide exactly into another number without a remainder.

What are the factors of 24?

1 is a factor of every number and so is the number itself (in this case, 24)	$1 \times 24 = 24$	1, 24
2 is a factor as 24 is even	$2 \times 12 = 24$	2, 12
3 is a factor as 3×8 is 24	$3 \times 8 = 24$	3, 8
4 is a factor as 4×6 is 24	$4 \times 6 = 24$	4, 6
5 is NOT a factor		
6 you already know is a factor so you can stop here.		

Answer The factors of 24 are 1, 2, 3, 4, 6, 8, 12 and 24

Highest common factors

Highest common factors (HCF) are the highest factors that are common to two numbers.

What is the highest common factor of 12 and 15?

The factors of 12 are 1, 2, 3, 4, 6 and 12.   The factors of 15 are 1, 3, 5 and 15.

Answer The highest common factor of 12 and 15 is 3

Multiples

A **multiple** is a number that is in a times table or beyond. Multiples of 5 are 5, 10, 15, 20, 25, 30... and continue beyond the times table, for example, 85, 115 and 500.

The answer to a multiplication question is a multiple of both the numbers multiplied. For example, $6 \times 7 = 42$ so 42 is a multiple of 6 and 7.

Multiples of 2, 4, 5, 8 and 10

- Multiples of 2 are even numbers (for example, 18, 34, 530, 416, 2002)
- Multiples of 4 are even when halved (like 12, 44, 760, 416, 2004)
- Multiples of 5 end in 0 or 5 (such as 10, 25, 415, 2010)
- Multiples of 8 are even when halved and halved again (like 32, 48, 680, 760, 2008)
  (Half 680 is 340, half 340 is 170. 170 is even, so 680 is a multiple of 8!)
- Multiples of 10 end in 0 (for example,10, 20, 410, 740, 2010).

Test yourself

1. How quickly can you answer these?
   8×3 9×4 7×4 7×8 3×7
2. Find all the factors of 96.
3. Which of these are multiples of 4?   92 740 114 214 242 332
4. What is the highest common factor of 18 and 24?

Remember

You will need to know your times tables to help you with factors and multiples. See page 40 for multiplication facts.

Multiples of 3, 6 and 9

- A number whose digits add up to a multiple of 3 is a multiple of 3, for example:

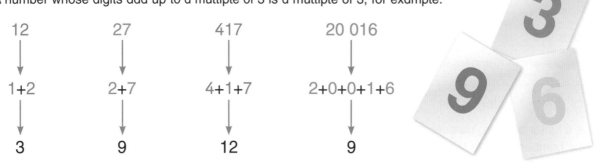

12	27	417	20 016
↓	↓	↓	↓
1+2	2+7	4+1+7	2+0+0+1+6
↓	↓	↓	↓
3	9	12	9

- An even number whose digits add up to a multiple of 3 is a multiple of 6 (such as 18, 42, 108, 31 314)
- A number whose digits add up to a multiple of 9 is a multiple of 9 (such as 36, 81, 216, 40 725).

Lowest common multiples

Lowest common multiples (LCM) are the lowest multiples that are common to two numbers.

> What is the lowest common multiple of 6 and 8?
>
> The first few multiples of 6 are 6, 12, 18 and 24.
> The first few multiples of 8 are 8, 16, 24 and 32.
>
> Answer The lowest common multiple of 6 and 8 is 24

Prime numbers

A **prime number** is a whole number that has only two factors, the number itself and 1 (like 2, 3, 5, 7, 11, 13, 17, 19, 23, 29...).

If a number is not prime it is called a **composite number**.

> What are the factors of 23?
>
> Ask, 'Which numbers divide into 23 without a remainder?'
>
> The only numbers that divide exactly into 23 without a remainder are 1 and 23.
>
> Answer 23 is a prime number.

Remember

Prime numbers have only two factors, the number itself and 1.

The number 1 is not a prime number, because it does not have two factors.

2 is the only even prime number.

Apart from the numbers 2 and 5, all primes end in 1, 3, 7 or 9. If a number ends in one of these numbers, use these tests to see if it has more than two factors. If it only has two, then it is a prime number.

- If a number is even it has the factor 2.
- If, when halved, the answer is even, it has the factor 4.
- If, when halved and halved again the answer is even, it has the factor 8.
- If a number ends in 0 it has the factor 10.
- If a number ends in 0 or 5 it has the factor 5.
- If the digits add up to a multiple of 3, it has the factor 3.
- If it's even and if the digits add up to a multiple of 3, it has the factor 6.
- If the digits add up to a multiple of 9 it has the factor 9.

Test yourself

1. Which of these are multiples of 6?   56 84 96 284 363 606

2. Which of these are multiples of 9?   117 186 379 459 702 969

3. Which of these are prime numbers?   67 69 73 89 95 107 473

4. What is the lowest common mulitple of 12 and 36?

Square numbers

Look at this number **sequence**.

1	4	9	16	25	36	49	64

   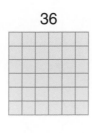 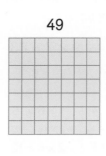 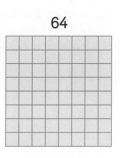

These are **square numbers**. Square numbers are created by squaring a number (multiplying a whole number by itself).

1^2 (1 squared) = 1 × 1 = 1

2^2 (2 squared) = 2 × 2 = 4

3^2 (3 squared) = 3 × 3 = 9

4^2 (4 squared) = 4 × 4 = 16

These are all square numbers.

Square roots

The number you multiply by itself to create a square number is called the **square root**. Finding the square root is the opposite of squaring.

You can use the √ key on a calculator to find the square root.

- The square root of 16 is 4, because 4 × 4 = 16
- The square root symbol is √ so $\quad$ √16 = 4
- The square root of 36 is 6, because 6 × 6 = 36 ⟶ √36 = 6
- The square root of 81 is 9, because 9 × 9 = 81 ⟶ √81 = 9

Which number, when multiplied by itself, gives 2209?

Press   to get the answer 47, because

47 × 47 = 2209

Answer 47

Test yourself

1. Cover up the rest of this page. Then write the sequence of the first 12 square numbers.
2. Answer these questions without a calculator. Which numbers, multiplied by themselves, give the answer:
   a 64 **b** 121 **c** 144?
3. Use a calculator to answer these.
   a Which number, multiplied by itself, gives 1521?
   b Which number, multiplied by itself, gives 3249?
   c What is the square root of 1681?
4. Which square number is closest to 5000?

Square numbers to 144

1	×	1	=	1
2	×	2	=	4
3	×	3	=	9
4	×	4	=	16
5	×	5	=	25
6	×	6	=	36
7	×	7	=	49
8	×	8	=	64
9	×	9	=	81
10	×	10	=	100
11	×	11	=	121
12	×	12	=	144

Remember

Learn the square numbers to 144! They are listed above.

Multiplication facts

Learn these tables facts and remember – if you know one fact you can just turn it around to get another. For example:

$$7 \times 9 = 63 \longleftrightarrow 9 \times 7 = 63$$

× 3	× 4	× 6	× 7	× 8	× 9	× 11	× 12
1 × 3 = 3	1 × 4 = 4	1 × 6 = 6	1 × 7 = 7	1 × 8 = 8	1 × 9 = 9	1 × 11 = 11	1 × 12 = 12
2 × 3 = 6	2 × 4 = 8	2 × 6 = 12	2 × 7 = 14	2 × 8 = 16	2 × 9 = 18	2 × 11 = 22	2 × 12 = 24
3 × 3 = 9	3 × 4 = 12	3 × 6 = 18	3 × 7 = 21	3 × 8 = 24	3 × 9 = 27	3 × 11 = 33	3 × 12 = 36
4 × 3 = 12	4 × 4 = 16	4 × 6 = 24	4 × 7 = 28	4 × 8 = 32	4 × 9 = 36	4 × 11 = 44	4 × 12 = 48
5 × 3 = 15	5 × 4 = 20	5 × 6 = 30	5 × 7 = 35	5 × 8 = 40	5 × 9 = 45	5 × 11 = 55	5 × 12 = 60
6 × 3 = 18	6 × 4 = 24	6 × 6 = 36	6 × 7 = 42	6 × 8 = 48	6 × 9 = 54	6 × 11 = 66	6 × 12 = 72
7 × 3 = 21	7 × 4 = 28	7 × 6 = 42	7 × 7 = 49	7 × 8 = 56	7 × 9 = 63	7 × 11 = 77	7 × 12 = 84
8 × 3 = 24	8 × 4 = 32	8 × 6 = 48	8 × 7 = 56	8 × 8 = 64	8 × 9 = 72	8 × 11 = 88	8 × 12 = 96
9 × 3 = 27	9 × 4 = 36	9 × 6 = 54	9 × 7 = 63	9 × 8 = 72	9 × 9 = 81	9 × 11 = 99	9 × 12 = 108
10 × 3 = 30	10 × 4 = 40	10 × 6 = 60	10 × 7 = 70	10 × 8 = 80	10 × 9 = 90	10 × 11 = 110	10 × 12 = 120
11 × 3 = 33	11 × 4 = 44	11 × 6 = 66	11 × 7 = 77	11 × 8 = 88	11 × 9 = 99	11 × 11 = 121	11 × 12 = 132
12 × 3 = 36	12 × 4 = 48	12 × 6 = 72	12 × 7 = 84	12 × 8 = 96	12 × 9 = 108	12 × 11 = 132	12 × 12 = 144

Learning multiplication facts

- Write down one fact a day and stick it somewhere you will often see it – like the fridge door or bathroom mirror.
- Use facts you know: if you know 7 × 6 = 42 then 8 × 6 will be 6 more than 42.
- As soon as you learn a fact, turn it round to learn the other: if you know 9 × 6 = 54 then 6 × 9 will also be 54.

$$9 \times 7 = 63$$

Test yourself

1. Cover up the tables grid and practise these.

8 × 5	5 × 8	8 × 9	9 × 8
3 × 6	6 × 3	3 × 11	11 × 3
7 × 3	3 × 7	7 × 8	8 × 7
6 × 8	8 × 6	7 × 7	12 × 12
9 × 4	4 × 9	11 × 11	6 × 6
4 × 12	12 × 4	8 × 8	9 × 9

Remember

When any number is multiplied by 0, the answer is always 0.

Division facts

Once you know your multiplication tables, division becomes easier too. If you know a tables fact, you automatically know two division facts. For example:

$$7 \times 9 = 63$$

$$63 \div 9 = 7 \qquad 63 \div 7 = 9$$

÷ 3	÷ 4	÷ 6	÷ 7	÷ 8	÷ 9	÷ 11	÷ 12
3 ÷ 3 = 1	4 ÷ 4 = 1	6 ÷ 6 = 1	7 ÷ 7 = 1	8 ÷ 8 = 1	9 ÷ 9 = 1	11 ÷ 11 = 1	12 ÷ 12 = 1
6 ÷ 3 = 2	8 ÷ 4 = 2	12 ÷ 6 = 2	14 ÷ 7 = 2	16 ÷ 8 = 2	18 ÷ 9 = 2	22 ÷ 11 = 2	24 ÷ 12 = 2
9 ÷ 3 = 3	12 ÷ 4 = 3	18 ÷ 6 = 3	21 ÷ 7 = 3	24 ÷ 8 = 3	27 ÷ 9 = 3	33 ÷ 11 = 3	36 ÷ 12 = 3
12 ÷ 3 = 4	16 ÷ 4 = 4	24 ÷ 6 = 4	28 ÷ 7 = 4	32 ÷ 8 = 4	36 ÷ 9 = 4	44 ÷ 11 = 4	48 ÷ 12 = 4
15 ÷ 3 = 5	20 ÷ 4 = 5	30 ÷ 6 = 5	35 ÷ 7 = 5	40 ÷ 8 = 5	45 ÷ 9 = 5	55 ÷ 11 = 5	60 ÷ 12 = 5
18 ÷ 3 = 6	24 ÷ 4 = 6	36 ÷ 6 = 6	42 ÷ 7 = 6	48 ÷ 8 = 6	54 ÷ 9 = 6	66 ÷ 11 = 6	72 ÷ 12 = 6
21 ÷ 3 = 7	28 ÷ 4 = 7	42 ÷ 6 = 7	49 ÷ 7 = 7	56 ÷ 8 = 7	63 ÷ 9 = 7	77 ÷ 11 = 7	84 ÷ 12 = 7
24 ÷ 3 = 8	32 ÷ 4 = 8	48 ÷ 6 = 8	56 ÷ 7 = 8	64 ÷ 8 = 8	72 ÷ 9 = 8	88 ÷ 11 = 8	96 ÷ 12 = 8
27 ÷ 3 = 9	36 ÷ 4 = 9	54 ÷ 6 = 9	63 ÷ 7 = 9	72 ÷ 8 = 9	81 ÷ 9 = 9	99 ÷ 11 = 9	108 ÷ 12 = 9
30 ÷ 3 = 10	40 ÷ 4 = 10	60 ÷ 6 = 10	70 ÷ 7 = 10	80 ÷ 8 = 10	90 ÷ 9 = 10	110 ÷ 11 = 10	120 ÷ 12 = 10
33 ÷ 3 = 11	44 ÷ 4 = 11	66 ÷ 6 = 11	77 ÷ 7 = 11	88 ÷ 8 = 11	99 ÷ 9 = 11	121 ÷ 11 = 11	132 ÷ 12 = 11
36 ÷ 3 = 12	48 ÷ 4 = 12	72 ÷ 6 = 12	84 ÷ 7 = 12	96 ÷ 8 = 12	108 ÷ 9 = 12	132 ÷ 11 = 12	144 ÷ 12 = 12

Learning division facts

- Write down one fact a day and stick it somewhere you will often see it – like the fridge door or bathroom mirror.
- Use the multiplication facts you know: if you know $8 \times 9 = 72$ then you know that $9 \times 8 = 72$. You also know that $72 \div 8 = 9$ and $72 \div 9 = 8$.
- Remove the picture cards from a pack of playing cards. Shuffle the remaining cards and turn them face down. Turn two over at a time. Multiply them, then write down both division facts.

$$56 \div 7 = 8$$

Test yourself

1. Cover up the division facts grid and practise these.

40 ÷ 5	27 ÷ 9	40 ÷ 8	27 ÷ 3
18 ÷ 6	121 ÷ 11	18 ÷ 3	144 ÷ 12
21 ÷ 3	56 ÷ 8	21 ÷ 7	56 ÷ 7
48 ÷ 12	108 ÷ 9	48 ÷ 4	108 ÷ 12
63 ÷ 7	49 ÷ 7	63 ÷ 9	9 ÷ 3
72 ÷ 9	64 ÷ 8	72 ÷ 8	81 ÷ 9

Remember

If you know a multiplication fact, you automatically know two division facts.

Mental multiplication

Multiplying by 10

To multiply by 10, move each digit one place to the left.

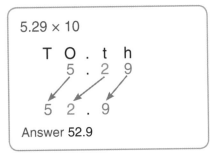

5.29 × 10

T O . t h
5 . 2 9
5 2 . 9

Answer 52.9

Multiplying by 100

To multiply by 100, move each digit two places to the left.

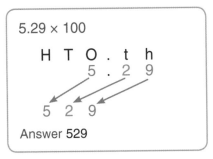

5.29 × 100

H T O . t h
5 . 2 9
5 2 9

Answer 529

Multiplying by 1000

To multiply by 1000, move each digit three places to the left.

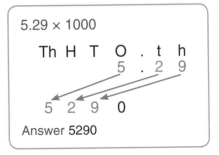

5.29 × 1000

Th H T O . t h
5 . 2 9
5 2 9 0

Answer 5290

Doubling

Doubling can help you to multiply numbers. To multiply a number:

- by 2 – just double it   → 34 × 2 → double 34 = 68
- by 4 – double and double again   → 16 × 4 → double 16 = 32
  double 32 = 64
- by 8 – double, double and double again → 19 × 8 → double 19 = 38
  double 38 = 76
  double 76 = 152

Using factors

Using **factors** (see page 37) can make multiplying in your head easier.

25 × 18

6 and 3 are factors of 18, so break 18 into 6 × 3, and the question becomes: 25 × 6 × 3

25 × 6 = 150 and 150 × 3 = 450, so 25 × 18 = 450

Answer 450

Remember

To multiply by 10, move each digit one place to the left.

To multiply by 100, move each digit two places to the left.

To multiply by 1000, move each digit three places to the left.

Splitting numbers

Make calculations easier by splitting numbers up as in the example below.

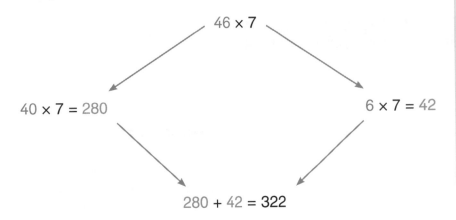

46 × 7

40 × 7 = 280   6 × 7 = 42

280 + 42 = 322

Test yourself

1. Multiply by 10.
   a 34
   b 809
   c 2853

2. Multiply by 100.
   a 24
   b 362
   c 4086

3. Double these numbers.
   a 17
   b 26
   c 39

4. Use doubling for these.
   a 24 × 4
   b 43 × 8

Mental division

Dividing by 10

To divide by 10, move each digit one place to the right.

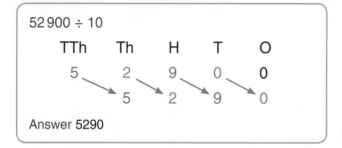

TTh	Th	H	T	O
5	2	9	0	0
	5	2	9	0

Answer 5290

Dividing by 100

To divide by 100, move each digit two places to the right.

52 900 ÷ 100

TTh	Th	H	T	O
5	2	9	0	0
		5	2	9

Answer 529

To divide by 1000, move each digit three places to the right.

Dividing decimal numbers by 10

Decimal numbers work in the same way.

To divide by 10, move each digit one place to the right.

68.3 ÷ 10

H	T	O	.	t	h	th
6	8	.	3			
	6	.	8	3		

Answer 6.83

Dividing decimal numbers by 100

To divide by 100, move each digit two places to the right.

68.3 ÷ 100

H	T	O	.	t	h	th
6	8	.	3			
	0	.	6	8	3	

Answer 0.683

Halving

Halving can help you to divide numbers. To divide a number:

- by 2 – just halve it $\longrightarrow$ 46 ÷ 2 $\longrightarrow$ half 46 = 23
- by 4 – halve and halve again $\longrightarrow$ 96 ÷ 4 $\longrightarrow$ half 96 = 48
  half 48 = 24
- by 8 – halve, halve and halve again $\longrightarrow$ 128 ÷ 8 $\longrightarrow$ half 128 = 64
  half 64 = 32
  half 32 = 16

Once you have learnt some doubles, you automatically know some halves.

- double 59 $\longrightarrow$ 118
- half 118 $\longrightarrow$ 59

Test yourself

1. Divide by 10.
   a 160 b 3840 c 645
2. Divide by 100.
   a 600 b 9700 c 35 200

3. Halve these numbers.
   a 68 b 78 c 96
4. Use halving for these.
   a 84 ÷ 2   c 104 ÷ 8
   b 88 ÷ 4

Remember

To divide by 10, move each digit one place to the right.

To divide by 100, move each digit two places to the right.

To divide by 1000, move each digit three places to the right.

Written multiplication

When you multiply, you should approximate first. Here are some different methods of written multiplication – you can choose any method you like.

Short multiplication

392×8

	Th	H	T	O
		3	9	2
×				8
	3	1	3	6
		3	7	1

Multiply each digit by 8 working from the right. If the answer to any part is more than 9, carry a digit across to the left.

24.7×6

H	T	O	.	t
	2	4	.	7
×				6
1	4	8	.	2
	2	4		

Multiply each digit by 6 working from the right. Make sure to keep the decimal point in the same place.

Long multiplication

1153×74

TTh	Th	H	T	O	
	1	1	5	3	
×			7	4	
	4	6$_2$	1$_1$	2	(×4)
8$_1$	0$_3$	7$_2$	1	0	(×70)
8	5$_1$	3	2	2	

Multiply 1153 first by the ones digit, 4, and then by the tens digit, 7, which stands for 70. Then add.

Multiplying decimals by decimals

Treat decimals in the same way as whole numbers, but:

- approximate first
- remember to put the **decimal point** in the answer!

Calculate 2.34×2.6

Approximation: $2 \times 3 = 6$ (then you needn't worry about the decimal points)

Now multiply as if they were whole numbers:

$$
\begin{array}{r}
234 \\
\times \quad 26 \\
\end{array}
$$

$234 \times 6 \longrightarrow 1404$

$234 \times 20 \longrightarrow 4680$

$\qquad\qquad\qquad 6084$

The answer must be 6.084 rather than 60.84 or 608.4 because our approximation was 6.

The total number of digits after the decimal points in the question will also be the same as the total number of digits after the decimal point in the answer.

$2.34 \times 2.6 \longrightarrow$ 3 digits in total after the decimal points

Answer 6.084

Remember

The process of multiplying is the same whatever size number you are multiplying. Just multiply each digit in turn, starting with the smallest value digit (the one furthest to the right).

Test yourself

1. Approximate first and then multiply these numbers.
   a 53×12
   b 257×18
   c 1305×27

2. Approximate first and then multiply these decimals.
   a 4.3×7
   b 4.9×9.5
   c 3.25×8

Written division

Here are some common ways of doing written division.

Short division
7425 ÷ 3

```
        2    4    7    5
  _____
3 ) 7   ¹4   ²2   ¹5
```

Work from left to right:

3 into 7 goes twice, write 2 above. Carry 1 to make 14.

3 into 14 goes 4 times. Write 4 above and carry 2 to make 22.

3 into 22 goes 7 times. Write 7 above and carry 1 to make 15.

3 into 15 goes 5 times.

Long division
685 ÷ 11

```
                    6    2    r 3
          _____
  1   1 | 6    8    5
      -   6    6
          _____
               2    5
          -    2    2
               _____
                    3
```

Work from left to right:

11 into 68 goes 6 times. Write 6 above. Multiply 11 by 6 and write 66 below. Subtract, 68 − 66 = 2. Bring down the next digit, 5.

11 into 25 goes 2 times. Write 2 above. Multiply 11 by 2 and write 22 below. Subtract, 25 − 22 = 3.

Answers with remainders

Some division answers are not whole numbers, as the numbers do not divide exactly. In these cases the answer can have a remainder, or a fraction to make a **mixed number**. Use the number you are dividing by (the divisor) as the **denominator** of the fraction and simplify if possible.

This long division 685 ÷ 11 (shown above) has the answer 62 r 3.

This can be changed to $62\frac{3}{11}$.

Test yourself

1. Approximate first and then divide these numbers.
- **a** 575 ÷ 5
- **b** 927 ÷ 9
- **c** 1560 ÷ 24
- **d** 12.5 ÷ 5
- **e** 82.2 ÷ 4
- **f** 53.55 ÷ 7

2. Write these as mixed numbers. Give fractions in their simplest form.
- **a** 464 ÷ 9 = 51 r 5
- **b** 172 ÷ 8 = 21 r 4
- **c** 800 ÷ 12 = 66 r 8
- **d** 766 ÷ 6 = 127 r 4

Remember

Division is easier if you know your division facts.

Order of operations

In maths there is an agreed order to do calculations that involve more than one operation (such as addition and multiplication).

The agreed order can be remembered using the word BODMAS, where each letter reminds you of the order.

Brackets ⟵ do anything in brackets first

Other ⟵ for example, squaring, cubing, powers or **square roots**

Divide ⎫
          ⎬ then divide or multiply numbers. Division and multiplication have equal weighting,
Multiply ⎭ even though division comes first in the word BODMAS. Whichever operation comes first in the calculation is the one you carry out first.

Add ⎫
       ⎬ finally add or subtract numbers. Addition and subtraction have equal weighting,
Subtract ⎭ even though addition comes first in the word BODMAS. Whichever operation comes first in the calculation is the one you carry out first.

Use BODMAS to help you answer this question: $9 + (5 + 3) \div 2^2 - 4 \times 2$

$9 + (5 + 3) \div 2^2 - 4 \times 2$	**B**rackets first
$9 + 8 \div 2^2 - 4 \times 2$	**O**ther things (like squaring) next
$9 + 8 \div 4 - 4 \times 2$	**D**ivide next
$9 + 2 - 4 \times 2$	**M**ultiply next
$9 + 2 - 8$	**A**dd next
$11 - 8$	**S**ubtract finally
Answer: **3**	

If a calculation only has one or two of these steps, you must still remember to do them in the correct order.

$3 \times (3 + 9) \div 6$

B
O
D
M
A
S

Test yourself

1. Answer these using BODMAS to help you.
- **a** $4 + 3 \times 5$
- **b** $(4 + 3) \times 5$
- **c** $9 \div 3 + 6$
- **d** $9 \div (3 + 6)$
- **e** $10 + 4 \times 2 - (6 - 5)$
- **f** $200 - 20 \div 5$
- **g** $(2 + 10) - 15 \div 3$
- **h** $5^2 + 7 \times 3^2$
- **i** $100 - 4 \times 2^2 - (7 - 3) \div 2$

Remember

Use BODMAS to make sure you carry out calculations in the correct order.

Word problems

When faced with a word problem:

- read it carefully
- write down important numbers
- decide how to work it out
- get an approximate answer, work it out, then check.

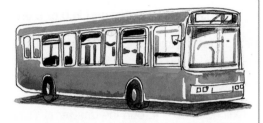

36 people were on the bus. At the bus stop 17 got off but 12 more got on. How many people were on the bus now?

Important numbers: 36, 17, 12

Subtract 17 from 36, and then add 12
Work it out: 36 −17 = 19, 19 + 12 = 31

Check against approximate answer.

Answer 31

Approximation: 40 − 20 + 10 = 30

Watch the units

Make sure all the numbers are in the same units before you **calculate**. Don't mix metres and centimetres, or litres and millilitres. Be particularly careful with pounds and pence – you shouldn't write both £ and p in your answers (for example, £5.87p).

Lucy pays £7.86 for 6 cupcakes to give to her friends. How much would she have paid for 27 cupcakes to give to the whole class?

Divide £7.86 by 6 to find the price of each cake.
Work it out: 786p ÷ 6 = 131p per cake

Multiply 131p by 27 to find the cost of 27 cakes.
Work it out: 131p × 27 = 3537p or £35.37

Check against approximate answer.

Answer £35.37

Approximation: 130 × 30 = 3900p or £39

Sunil buys a drink for 35p, crisps for 38p and a sandwich for £1.45. He buys the same drink, crisps and sandwich every day for 3 days. How much does he spend?

In one day, he spends 35p + 38p + 145p = 218p

Multiply 218p by 3 to find the cost over 3 days. Work it out: 218p × 3 = 654p or £6.54

Check against approximate answer.

Answer £6.54

Approximation: 40p + 40p + 150p = 230p, 230p × 3 = 690p or £6.90

Test yourself

1. Laptops are usually £392 each. In the sale there is a discount of £54 on each laptop. What is the new price?
2. 27 people were on the bus. When it stopped, 18 more got on and 23 got off. How many are on the bus now?
3. Tom buys a hot chocolate for £1.12, adds peppermint syrup for 39p and marshmallows for 72p. How much does he spend?

Remember

Make sure the numbers are in the same units before you calculate.

Remainders in problem solving

When you are solving a problem that involves division, watch out for remainders. Remainders happen because numbers are not always exactly divisible by other numbers.

- All whole numbers are exactly divisible by 1.
- All even numbers are exactly divisible by 2.
- All odd numbers will have a remainder of 1 when divided by 2.
- All whole numbers that end in 0 are exactly divisible by 10.
- All whole numbers that end in 0 or 5 are exactly divisible by 5.

See pages 37 and 38 for more information on dividing without remainders.

> How many 4s in 46?
>
> Calculate 46 ÷ 4, and the answer is 11 remainder 2
>
> Answer 11 r 2

46 children are going on a trip. Each car carries four children. How many cars are needed?

Which is right?

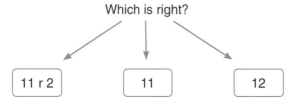

| 11 r 2 | 11 | 12 |

Although there will be only two children in the 12th car, that car is still needed.

Answer 12

46 photos are in a photo album, with four on each page. How many pages are full?

Which is right?

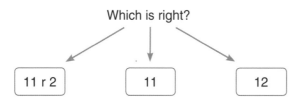

| 11 r 2 | 11 | 12 |

Only 11 pages are full, because 11 × 4 = 44, with two spare photos.

Answer 11

Test yourself

1. A postman has 356 letters to deliver. He can fit 100 letters in his bag. How many trips will he have to make?
2. The football club has £60 to buy footballs. Each football costs £8. How many can it buy?
3. I have 160 biscuits to put in boxes. One box holds 35 biscuits.
   a How many boxes can I fill?
   b How many boxes will I need?

Remember

Watch out for remainders and think carefully about what they mean. Sometimes you may need to round up or down.

Missing number problems

The boxes show the calculations you can do to find each missing number.

$50 +$ ☐ $= 101$ $12 -$ ☐ $= 3$ ☐ $\times 5 = 20$ $70 \div$ ☐ $= 10$

| $101 - 50 = 51$ | | $12 - 3 = 9$ | $20 \div 5 = 4$ | | $70 \div 10 = 7$ |

Finding the largest number

A good way to answer questions using positive whole numbers is to think about the largest number:

- in addition and multiplication questions, the answer is always the largest number
- in subtraction and division questions, the first number is always the largest number.

So first, find the largest number. Then decide whether the missing number is larger or smaller than the other numbers.

- If it is smaller, use the other numbers to make it smaller, by subtracting or dividing.
- If it is larger, use the other numbers to make it larger, by adding or multiplying.

 $- 87 = 38$

The first number is the largest. This is the missing number.

You can use the other two numbers to make this largest number by adding 87 to 38.

Answer 125

$703 \div$ ☐ $= 19$

The first number is the largest, so the missing number is smaller.

Now you use the other two numbers to make a smaller number by dividing 703 by 19.

Answer 37

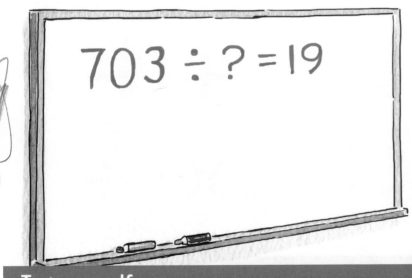

$$703 \div ? = 19$$

Test yourself

1. Find the missing numbers.

   a $45 +$ 41 $= 86$ **c** ☐ $\times 7 = 42$ **e** $50 \div$ ☐ $= 2.5$

   b $25 -$ 13 $= 12$ **d** $65 \div$ ☐ $= 5$ **f** ☐ $\times 36 = 216$

2. Now try these more difficult ones.

   a $315 +$ ☐ $= 1001$ **b** $8 \times$ ☐ $= 536$

Remember

With positive whole numbers:
+ and × make numbers bigger;
− and ÷ make numbers smaller.

Checking answers

When checking calculations you can use approximations or rounding to see if an answer is 'about right'.

$$7946 - 4866 = 3080$$

Approximation: $8000 - 5000 = 3000$

You can also use inverse operations to check your answer.

- To check an addition, subtract the number added from your answer.
- To check a subtraction, add the number subtracted to your answer.
- To check a multiplication, divide the answer by a number in the question.
- To check a division, multiply your answer by a number in the question.

$7946 - 4866 = 3080$

To check this, add the number subtracted, 4866, to the answer 3080.

$$
\begin{array}{r}
4866 \\
+ 3080 \\
\hline
7946 \\
\end{array}
$$
1

If the calculation gives the other number in each question, it is correct.

$3888 \div 8 = 486$

To check this, multiply the answer by one number from the question to give the other number.

$$
\begin{array}{r}
486 \\
\times \quad 8 \\
\hline
3888 \\
\end{array}
$$
$6\,4$

Addition and subtraction are opposites.

| $12 - 7 = 5$ | $5 + 7 = 12$ | $12 - 5 = 7$ |

Multiplication and division are opposites.

| $12 \div 4 = 3$ | $3 \times 4 = 12$ | $12 \div 3 = 4$ |

These operations are opposites because they 'undo' each other.

Test yourself

1. Check each of these calculations using approximation and inverses. Which of the answers below are correct?

   a $453 + 533 = 986$

   b $365 - 50 = 287$

   c $11 \times 45 = 855$

   d $1288 \div 23 = 56$

   e $2016 \div 11 = 63$

   f $0.9 \times 28 = 25.2$

   g $578.5 \div 6.5 = 89$

   h $27 \times 5 = 86.4$

Remember

Addition is the inverse of subtraction. Multiplication is the inverse of division.

Formulae

A formula is a way of writing a mathematical rule that helps you to find answers quickly.
Here are some formulae you may already know:

area of a rectangle = length × width

volume of a cuboid = length × width × height

Look at these questions:

How many days are there in three weeks?	How many days are there in six weeks?	How many days are there in 50 weeks?

You can use a formula to help answer these questions.

number of days = $7 \times n$ or number of days = $7n$

The letter n stands for the number of weeks. To answer the questions, you just swap n for the number of weeks.

> How many days are there in three weeks?
>
> Number of days = $7 \times n$
>
> $\qquad 7 \times 3 = 21$
>
> Answer **21 days**

> How many days are there in six weeks?
>
> Number of days = $7 \times n$
>
> $\qquad 7 \times 6 = 42$
>
> Answer **42 days**

Using a formula

At a fair, the entrance fee is £3 and each ride costs £2.

The formula for the cost in pounds (c) of entering the fair and going on n rides is:

$$c = 3 + 2n$$

cost in pounds   entrance fee   2 × the number of rides

How much would it cost to enter the fair and go on five rides?

$n = 5$
$c = 3 + (2 \times 5)$
$c = 3 + 10$
$c = 13$

Answer **£13**

Remember

When a letter is next to a number it means they are multiplied together: $7n$ means $7 \times n$.

Test yourself

1. Use the formula to find the days in:
   a 50 weeks
   b 75 weeks
   c 83 weeks
   d 97 weeks
   e 100 weeks.

2. Look at the question about the fair at the bottom of this page. How much would it cost to enter the fair and go on:
   a 7 rides
   b 10 rides
   c 15 rides
   d 25 rides
   e 100 rides?

Number sequences and equations

Number sequences

A number sequence may be expressed as a formula which will help you to determine a number in any position in the sequence. Look at this example:

   3   5   7   9   11

Whilst you could say that the rule is +2, this may not help if you need to give the 100th number in the sequence. Knowing that the formula is $2n + 1$ (with n representing the position of the number in the sequence), then $2 \times 100 + 1 = 201$. The 100th number will be 201.

To work out what the formula would be, you need to work out how the first number in the sequence has been created and then see if the second and third numbers are created in the same way. By looking at the difference between each number, you can often find what you need to multiply the number by.

What is the formula for this sequence?

   5   8   11   14   17

The numbers are going up in 3s so the formula may begin $3n$. If 1 (the position of the first number) is multiplied by 3 you would still need to add 2 to get 5 so the formula would be $3n + 2$. This works with the second number as $3 \times 2 + 2 = 8$, and the third, $3 \times 3 + 2 = 11$. Therefore, the formula for this sequence is definitely $3n + 2$.

Answer $3n + 2$

Equations

Equations contain an equals symbol (=).

Sometimes an equation will have a variety of possible answers.

__ + __ = 5	$2g + w = 10$
$0 + 5 = 5$	If $g = 0$, $w = 10$
$1 + 4 = 5$	If $g = 1$, $w = 8$
$2 + 3 = 5$	If $g = 2$, $w = 6$
$3 + 2 = 5$	If $g = 3$, $w = 4$
$4 + 1 = 5$	If $g = 4$, $w = 2$
$5 + 0 = 5$	If $g = 5$, $w = 0$

On other occasions there will be a specific answer.

$y + 2 = 7$ by subtracting 2 from both sides of the equation you can work out that $y = 5$

What is the value of y?

$y - 3 = 8$ by adding 3 to both sides of the equation you can see that $y = 11$

> **Remember**
>
> Letters and symbols are used in algebra in the place of numbers that are unknown and other variables.

> **Test yourself**
>
> 1. What will the 50th number in the sequence be? The formula is given in brackets.
>   a 3   7   11   15   19
> $(4n - 1)$
>   b 8   10   12   14   16
> $(2n + 6)$
>
> 2. What are the formulae for the following sequences?
>   a 5   7   9   11   13
>   b 2   7   12   17   22
>
> 3. What are the possible numbers that could complete this equation?
> $3d + e = 13$

Metric units

When you are measuring, it is important to know what units and what instruments to use. There are different units and instruments, depending on whether you are measuring length, time, **capacity**, mass, area, **volume**, angles or temperature.

Most things today are measured in metric units, such as centimetres or kilograms.

You will need to know these metric units.

Type of measurement	Units (metric)	Instruments
Length (including height, width, depth, perimeter, distance)	millimetres (mm), centimetres (cm), metres (m), kilometres (km)	ruler, tape measure, trundle wheel, metre stick
Time	seconds, minutes, hours, days, weeks, years, decades	watch, clock, timer, stopwatch
Capacity	millilitres (ml), centilitres (cl), litres (l)	measuring jugs, cylinders
Mass (weight)	grams (g), kilograms (kg)	balance, kitchen and bathroom scales
Area	centimetre squares (cm^2), metre squares (m^2)	squares, grids
Volume	centimetre cubes (cm^3), metre cubes (m^3)	cubes
Angle	degrees (°)	protractor/angle measurer
Temperature	degrees Celsius (°C)	thermometer

Test yourself

1. Cover up the table above. What units would you use to measure:
   a time
   b length
   c mass (weight)
   d capacity
   e area
   f volume
   g temperature
   h angle?

Remember

Always write the units you are using. Use the word mass instead of weight when measuring in grams and kilograms.

Converting between metric units

You need to know how many of one unit makes up another.

Length
10mm = 1cm
100cm = 1m
1000m = 1km

Mass
1000g = 1kg
1000kg = 1 tonne

Time
60 seconds = 1 minute
60 minutes = 1 hour
24 hours = 1 day
7 days = 1 week
14 days = 1 fortnight
52 weeks = 1 year
365 or 366 days = 1 year
10 years = 1 decade
100 years = 1 century

Capacity
1000ml = 1l
100cl = 1l
10ml = 1cl

Use these diagrams to help you **convert** between metric units.

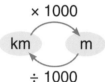 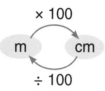 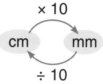 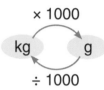

× 1000	× 100	× 10	× 1000	× 1000
km → m	m → cm	cm → mm	l → ml	kg → g
÷ 1000	÷ 100	÷ 10	÷ 1000	÷ 1000

If you're having difficulty multiplying and dividing by 10, 100 and 1000, see pages 42–43.

Convert 56m to centimetres

× 100
56m → cm
÷ 100

56 × 100 = 5600

Answer 5600cm

Convert 8675g to kilograms

× 1000
kg ← 8675g
÷ 1000

8675 ÷ 1000 = 8.675

Answer 8.675kg

Convert 92l to millilitres

× 1000
92l → ml
÷ 1000

92 × 1000 = 92 000

Answer 92 000ml

Test yourself

Cover up the conversion tables.

1. a 100cm =   **d** 1kg =   **2.** Convert the following.
   b 52 weeks =   **e** 1km =   **a** 35m to cm   **d** 7l to ml
   c 1000ml =   **f** 10 years =   **b** 750cm to m   **e** 2500g to kg
                                        c 6520ml to l   **f** 3.25kg to g

Remember

'Centi' stands for a hundredth (100 centimetres in a metre).

'Milli' stands for a thousandth (1000 millimetres in a metre).

'Kilo' stands for one thousand (1000 metres in a kilometre).

Imperial units

Imperial units are used less often than metric units, but they were once the only units used.
Metric units were introduced because they are easier to use. You will need to know these imperial units.

Measurements	Units (imperial)
Length (including height, width, depth, perimeter, distance)	inches, feet, yards, miles
Capacity	pints, gallons
Mass (weight)	ounces, pounds, stones

Converting between imperial units

It is useful to know how many of one unit makes up another unit.

Length
12 inches = 1 foot
3 feet = 1 yard
1760 yards = 1 mile

Capacity
8 pints = 1 gallon

Mass (weight)
16 ounces (oz) = 1 pound
14 pounds (lb) = 1 stone

Converting between metric and imperial units

It is also useful to know the relationships between metric and imperial units.

Length
2.5cm is about 1 inch
30cm (a long ruler) is about 1 foot
90cm is about 1 yard
1.6km is about 1 mile

Mass (weight)
25g is about 1 ounce
400g is about 1 pound
1kg is about 2.2 pounds
6kg is about 1 stone

Capacity
500ml ($\frac{1}{2}$ litre) is about 1 pint
4.5 litres is about 1 gallon

Test yourself

1. Cover up the rest of this page. Complete these sentences.
   a Imperial units for length include...
   b Imperial units for capacity include...
   c Imperial units for mass include...

2. a 1 foot = ____ inches
   b 1 mile = ____ yards
   c 1 stone = ____ pounds
   d 1 gallon = ____ pints
   e 1 pound = ____ ounces
   f 1 yard = ____ feet

3. a 1 foot is about ____ cm
   b 1lb is about ____ g
   c 1 mile is about ____ km
   d 1 gallon is about ____ l
   e 1oz is about ____ g
   f 1 yard is about ____ cm

Remember

Learn the names of imperial units, their abbreviations and roughly what they are worth in terms of metric units.

Perimeter

Perimeter is the distance around the outside of a 2-D shape. It is measured in centimetres (cm), metres (m) or kilometres (km).

Imagine walking around this playground. How far will you walk to get back to where you started?

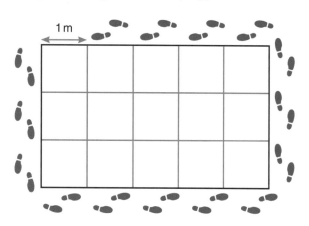

Trace your route, counting as you go.

The total distance would be 16m, so the perimeter is 16m.

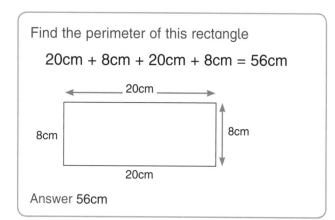

Find the perimeter of this rectangle

20cm + 8cm + 20cm + 8cm = 56cm

Answer 56cm

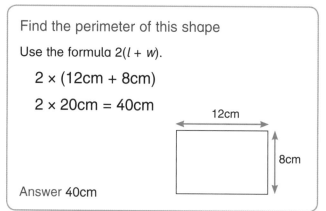

Find the perimeter of this shape

Use the formula 2(l + w).

2 × (12cm + 8cm)

2 × 20cm = 40cm

Answer 40cm

The opposite sides of a rectangle are the same length. This means you can find the perimeter when given only two sides.

The perimeter is:

15cm + 15cm + 10cm + 10cm = 50cm or 2 × 15cm + 2 × 10cm = 50cm

You can write this as a formula in different ways:

2 × length + 2 × width or $2l + 2w$ or $2(l + w)$

Test yourself

1. Find the perimeter of these shapes.

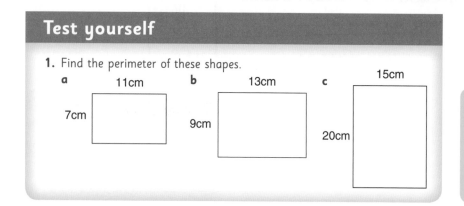

Remember

l stands for length, w stands for width. The formula for finding the perimeter of a rectangle is:

$2(l + w)$

Perimeters of other shapes

Find the perimeter of these shapes

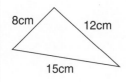

Add the lengths of the three sides.

Perimeter = 8cm + 12cm + 15cm

Answer 35cm

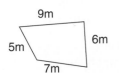

Add the lengths of the four sides.

Perimeter = 9m + 6m + 7m + 5m

Answer 27m

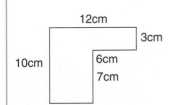

Add the lengths of the sides.

12cm + 3cm + 6cm + 7cm + 6cm + 10cm

Answer 44cm

Shapes with missing lengths

Sometimes you have to work out the lengths of some of the sides before you can find the **perimeter**.

Find the perimeter of this shape

There are two sides with no lengths given.

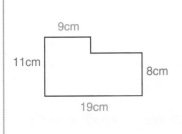

Find them by subtracting:

19cm − 9cm =10cm
11cm − 8cm = 3cm

Add the lengths of the sides:

11cm + 9cm + 3cm + 10cm
+ 8cm + 19cm = 60cm

Answer 60cm

The perimeter of a rectangle is 36cm. The shortest side is 6cm. What is the length of the longest side?

Draw a rectangle. Mark the two 6cm sides.

6cm + 6cm = 12cm

36cm − 12cm = 24cm

6cm   6cm

24cm is how much is left for the other two sides.
So they must be 12cm each.

Answer 12cm

Remember

To find the perimeters of shapes like these, add up the lengths of all the sides.

Test yourself

1. Find the perimeter of these shapes.

   a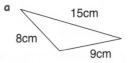

   b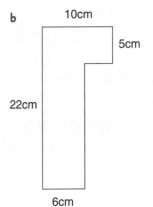

2. The perimeter of a rectangle is 48cm. The longest side is 19cm. What is the length of the shortest side?

Area

Area is the amount of surface that a shape covers.

In a 2-D (flat) shape, it is the space inside the lines or within a boundary.

In a 3-D (solid) shape, it is the total amount of surface of all the **faces**. This is called **surface area**.

Area is measured in square units, such as square millimetres (mm²), square centimetres (cm²), square metres (m²) and square kilometres (km²). The 2 in the squared sign can help you remember that you need to multiply the lengths of the two dimensions (length × width).

Finding area by counting squares

You can find the area of a rectangle by counting the number of squares it covers.

Find the area of this rectangle

The area is 12 centimetre squares.

1cm

1cm

Answer area = 12cm²

Finding area by multiplying

The rectangle above has 3 rows with 4 squares in each. 3 × 4 is 12. The area is 12cm².

Find the area of this rectangle without counting all the squares

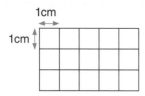

1cm

1cm

Count the number of squares along the top (5) and the side (3).

5cm × 3cm = 15cm².

Answer area = 15cm²

Find the area of this rectangle

Here the measurements are given for two of the sides.

8cm

5cm

Use this formula:

area of a rectangle = length × width

or $A = l \times w$

$A = 8cm \times 5cm = 40cm^2$

Answer area = 40cm²

Test yourself

1. Find the area of these rectangles.

a 5cm 4cm

b 10mm 6mm

c 7cm 13cm

Remember

A square with sides 1m has an area of 1m². 1m × 1m = 1m²

The same square measured in cm has an area of 10 000cm². 100cm × 100cm = 10 000cm² 1m² = 10 000cm²

Areas of parallelograms and triangles

The area of a parallelogram can be found by multiplying its length by its vertical height.
Notice how the parts can be rearranged to make a rectangle.

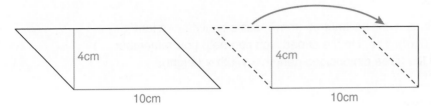

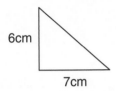

area of parallelogram =
4cm × 10cm = 40cm

The areas of triangles can be found by finding half of the area of a rectangle.

6cm

7cm

$$\text{area of triangle} = \tfrac{1}{2} \text{ length} \times \text{width}$$
$$= \tfrac{1}{2}(6cm \times 7cm)$$
$$= \tfrac{1}{2} \times 42cm^2$$
$$= 21cm^2$$

Areas of other shapes

This compound shape is made from two rectangles joined together. This can help you to work out the area of the shape.

8cm

12cm

6cm

15cm

Remember

A triangle is like half a rectangle. You can use this to find the area of a triangle: $\tfrac{1}{2} l \times w$

Find the area of this compound shape

Split into two rectangles.

Find the area of each, then add the areas together.

6cm × 7cm =   42cm²
8cm × 12cm =   96cm²
              138cm²

Answer area = 138cm²

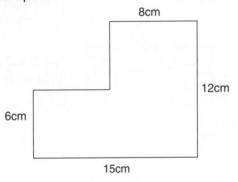

Test yourself

1. Find the area of these shapes.

a

7cm

12cm

b

15cm

8cm

c

16cm

10cm

6cm

4cm

Find the area of this compound shape

Split into two rectangles.

14cm × 6cm =   84cm²
5cm × 4cm =   20cm²
              104cm²

Answer area = 104cm²

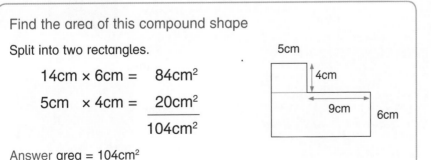

5cm

4cm

9cm

6cm

Volume

Volume is the space inside a 3-D shape.

Volume is measured in cubic units, such as cubic millimetres (mm^3), cubic centimetres (cm^3), cubic metres (m^3) and cubic kilometres (km^3). The 3 in the cubed sign can help you remember that you need to multiply the lengths of the three dimensions (length × width × height).

Finding volume by counting cubes

To find the volume of a cuboid, follow these steps.

- First count the cubes in one layer.
- Then count the number of layers.
- Multiply the number of cubes in one layer (8) by the number of layers (2).

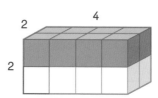

8 cubes
1cm
2 layers

$8 \times 2 = 16$
volume = $16cm^3$

> **Remember**
>
> volume of a cuboid = length (l) × width (w) × height (h)
>
> You can multiply the three numbers in any order – the answer will be the same.

Finding volume using length, width and height

Look at the shape again. Count the number of cubes along its height, length and width:
length = 4, width = 2, height = 2

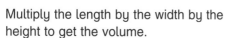

4
2
2

Multiply the length by the width by the height to get the volume.

$4 \times 2 \times 2 = 16$
volume = $16cm^3$

Find the volume of this cuboid without counting all the cubes

Multiply $l \times w \times h$

$4 \times 3 \times 3 = 36$

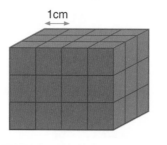

1cm

Answer volume = $36cm^3$

Find the volume of this cuboid

Multiply the length by the width by the height:

$10 \times 5 \times 8 = 400$

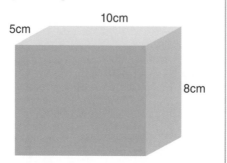

5cm
10cm
8cm

Answer volume = $400cm^3$

Test yourself

1. Find the volume of these cuboids.

   a
   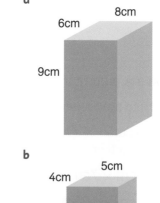
   8cm
   6cm
   9cm

   b
   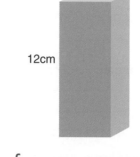
   5cm
   4cm
   12cm

   c
   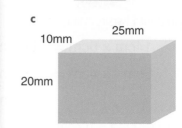
   25mm
   10mm
   20mm

Capacity

The **capacity** of something is the amount it can hold. It is measured in millilitres (ml) and litres (l) and in imperial units (pints and gallons).

A millilitre is a small amount of liquid that fills about $\frac{1}{5}$ of a teaspoon.

A litre is a much larger quantity of liquid – the amount found in a standard pack of juice.

Remember 1000ml = 1 litre. Use this diagram to **convert** between litres and millilitres (ml).

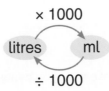

× 1000

litres → ml

÷ 1000

Measuring capacity

You can measure capacity in containers that have scales marked on them. Look at page 62 for help in reading scales.

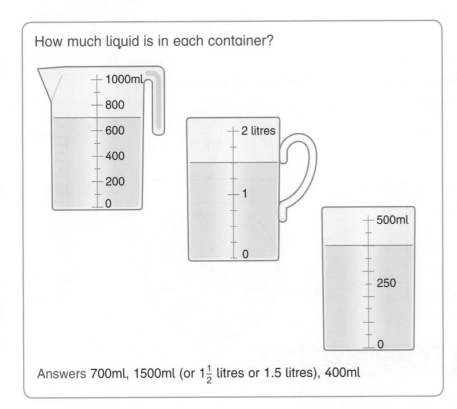

How much liquid is in each container?

Answers 700ml, 1500ml (or $1\frac{1}{2}$ litres or 1.5 litres), 400ml

Remember

1ml of water is equivalent to 1cm³. 50ml and 50cm³ take up the same amount of space.

Test yourself

1. What could you measure in:
   a millilitres
   b pints
   c litres
   d gallons?

2. Estimate the capacity of:
   a a bucket
   b an egg cup
   c a mug
   d a teapot
   e a bath.

3. Change these amounts to millilitres.
   a 7 litres
   b 8.5 litres

4. Change these amounts to litres.
   a 500ml
   b 4575ml

Linking volume and capacity

Sometimes units of volume, like cubic centimetres (cm³) and cubic metres (m³), are used to describe capacity. This is because 1 litre of water is equivalent to 1000cm³ and 1 millilitre of water is equivalent to 1cm³.

1cm cube

Reading scales

The key to reading scales on measuring instruments is to look carefully at the numbers on the scale and to follow these steps.

1. Choose two **adjacent** numbers (next to each other) and find the difference between them.

2. Count how many small intervals (spaces) there are between these numbers.

3. Work out, by dividing, how much each of these intervals is worth.

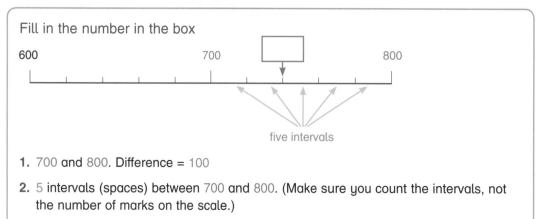

Fill in the number in the box

1. 700 and 800. Difference = 100

2. 5 intervals (spaces) between 700 and 800. (Make sure you count the intervals, not the number of marks on the scale.)

3. 100 ÷ 5 = 20

Each interval is 20, so the arrow is pointing to 740 (700 + 20 + 20).

Answer 740

Practising reading scales

Practise reading the scales below. Write down your readings, then check the answers (in the back of this book) to see if they are correct.

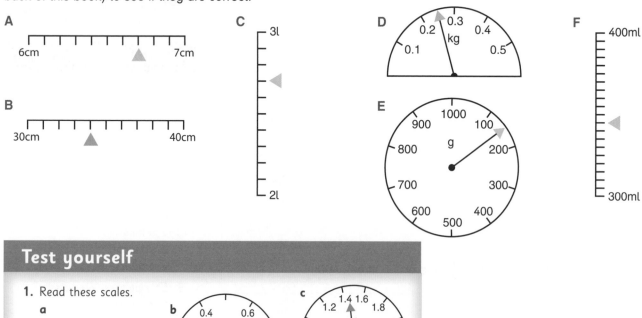

Test yourself

1. Read these scales.

   a   b   c   d

Remember

When reading scales, remember to write down the units you are measuring in.

Time

Time is measured in seconds (s), minutes (min), hours (hr), days, weeks, months, years and centuries.

60 seconds = 1 minute
60 minutes = 1 hour
24 hours = 1 day
7 days = 1 week
52 weeks = 1 year
365 days = 1 year

366 days = 1 leap year
12 months = 1 year
10 years = 1 decade
100 years = 1 century
1000 years = 1 millennium

Converting between units of time

Use the diagrams below to change between units of time.

Change 4 days into hours

Choose the correct diagram and insert the number.

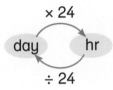

$4 \times 24 = 96$

Answer 96 hours

Change 540 seconds into minutes

Choose the correct diagram and insert the number.

$540 \div 60 = 9$

Answer 9 minutes

Days in the month

To remember the number of days in each month learn this rhyme:

30 days have September, April, June and November,
All the rest have 31, save February alone,
Which has 28 clear and 29 in each leap year.

Test yourself

1. Cover up the table of units and complete these.
   a 24 hours =
   b 52 weeks =
   c 10 years =
   d 60 minutes =
   e 100 years =
   f 60 seconds =

2. Convert:
   a 5 days to hours
   b 420 minutes to hours
   c 8 minutes to seconds
   d 7 hours to minutes.

Remember

When looking at two equivalent times (such as 4 days and 96 hours), the smaller unit (hours) will have the larger number (96), and the larger unit (days) will have the smaller number (4).

12-hour clocks

If you are using a 12-hour clock, you must always write a.m. or p.m., for example 11.20 p.m. (evening) or 11.20 a.m. (morning).

This is because the hands of a 12-hour clock go round twice in one day, and you need to show which part of the day you mean:

- a.m. is for times between midnight and midday (morning)
- p.m. is for times between midday and midnight (afternoon and evening).

24-hour clocks

A 24-hour clock uses the numbers from 0 to 24 to stand for all the hours in the day. 0 is midnight, and after midday the hours become 13, 14, 15, 16 and so on. For example, 5 p.m. is shown as 17:00 and 9.30 p.m. as 21:30.

If you are using the 24-hour clock, you must always write the time using four digits, for example 16:45 or 09:10.

Telling the time with 12- and 24-hour clocks

Many clocks today are digital – they show the time using digits.

Some clocks and watches are analogue – they show the time on a circular face using hands.

12-hour clock	Analogue clockface	24-hour clock

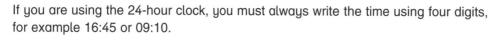

quarter to seven in the morning	quarter to seven	six forty-five

twenty past nine in the evening	twenty past nine	twenty-one twenty

Test yourself

1. Which of these are correct?
   a six thirty in the morning is 6.30 p.m.
   b eight fifteen in the evening is 8.15 p.m.
   c ten past four in the afternoon is 4.10 p.m.
   d quarter to ten in the morning is 9.45 p.m.
2. Convert these times to 24-hour times.
   a 8.20 a.m. b 12.15 p.m. c 3.35 a.m. d 1.05 p.m.
3. Convert these times to a.m. and p.m. times.
   a 16:54   b 08:00   c 12:29   d 19:20

Remember

If you are using the 12-hour clock you must always write a.m. or p.m.

If you are using the 24-hour clock you must always write the time using four digits.

Calculating with time

You may be asked to find how long a programme or event goes on for and when it started or finished.
Don't use a calculator when dealing with time – you will get the wrong answer!

If a film starts at 7.20 p.m. and goes on for 1 hour 45 minutes, what time does it end?

Add or subtract the whole hours first, and then count on or count back the extra minutes.

7.20 p.m. + 1 hour   ⟶   8.20 p.m.

Then count on 45min   ⟶   9.05 p.m.

Answer 9.05 p.m.

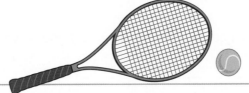

Black Knight

Sceen 10	Seat L14	Child £4.20

CINEMA

Time	Duration	Date
19.30	1h 45min	14/05/2016

T I C K E T

If a tennis match lasts for 2 hours 40 minutes and ends at 1.25 p.m., what time did it start?

1.25 p.m. – 2 hours   ⟶   11.25 a.m.

Then count back 40min   ⟶   10.45 a.m.

Answer 10.45 a.m.

If the time now is 17:27, what time will it be in 3 hours 20 minutes?

17:27 + 3 hours ⟶ 20:27 then count on 20 min ⟶ 20:47.

Answer 20:47

Here are the start and finish times of some runners in a marathon

Name	Start time	Finish time
Tom	10:20	14:35
Sara	10:25	14:05
Sajid	10:30	13:20

How much longer did Sara take than Sajid?

Find how long Sara and Sajid took.

Sajid took 2hrs 50min and Sara took 3hrs 40min.

Count on in minutes from 2hrs 50min to 3hrs 40min.

Answer Sara took 50 minutes longer.

Test yourself

1. If a TV programme starts at 1.20 p.m. and goes on for 3 hours 10 minutes, at what time does it end?
2. If I walk for 4 hours and 20 minutes, stopping at 13:35, at what time did I start?
3. If the time now is 7.15 a.m., what time will it be in 2 hours 40 minutes?
4. If the time now is 03:20, what time was it 5 hours 10 minutes ago?

Remember

Add or subtract the whole hours first and then count on or count back the extra minutes.

Timetables

Timetables are lists that give information about when things happen, such as train or bus times, TV programmes, cinema times, and so on.

The 24-hour clock is often used in timetables to avoid confusion over a.m. and p.m. To read a timetable, look along a row and down a column to find where they meet.

When does 'Black Knight' start at the Filmhouse?

Read across the row from Black Knight and down the column from the Filmhouse.

CINEMA TIMES FOR THURSDAY			
	Academy	Silver Screen	*Filmhouse*
Happy Days	14:20	15:45	17:50
The Game	19:50	20:40	21:40
Black Knight	18:30	19:45	19:30
The Shore	20:20	21:20	21:15

Answer Black Knight starts at 19:30.

Look at the timetable below. Which train would you catch from Hawkser to arrive at Ashby at 11:00?

	TRAIN 1	TRAIN 2	TRAIN 3	TRAIN 4
Hawkser	08:30	09:45	12:00	14:30
Scarby	08:45	10:00	12:15	14:45
Egton	09:30	10:30	12:45	15:15
Ashby	10:00	11:00	13:30	16:00

Look across from Ashby to 11:00. What time is that train at Hawkser?

Answer 09:45

Which train would you catch from Scarby to arrive at Egton at 12:45?

Look across from Egton to 12:45. What time is that train at Scarby?

Answer 12:15

Which train would you catch from Hawkser to be in Egton at 15:00?

The 14:30 would arrive too late, so you would catch the 12:00.

Answer the 12:00 train

Test yourself

1. When does 'The Game' start at the Academy?
2. What is the earliest time you can see 'Happy Days'?
3. What is the latest time you can see 'Black Knight'?
4. Which train would you catch from Scarby to arrive at Ashby at 16:00?
5. Which train would you catch from Hawkser to be in Ashby at 13:00?
6. Which is the fastest train?

Remember

To read a timetable, look along a row and down a column to where these meet.

Measurement problems

Measurement problems will often contain mixed units. Change them so that they are all the same.

Adam had a piece of wood that was 3.5m long. He cut as many 15cm pieces off as he could. How long was the final piece he was left with?

The question has metres and centimetres, so convert the metres to centimetres to keep all the units the same. 3.5m = 350cm

350cm ÷ 15cm = 23r5 so he would be able to cut 23 pieces at 15cm with a 5cm piece left over.

Answer 5cm

Mali counted all of the money in her money boxes. There was 167p in her piggy bank, £12.83 in her unicorn money box and 493p in a large bottle. She needs £20 to buy a new pair of trainers. How much more money does she need?

The question has pence and pounds, so convert the pence to pounds to keep all the units the same.

$$£1.67 + £12.83 + £4.93 = £19.43$$

$$£20 - £19.43 = £0.57$$

Answer 57p

Tomas made a clay model of his cat. The model weighed 4.5 times less than his actual cat. If the model weighed 1.21kg, how much did his cat weigh?

$$1.21 \times 4.5 = 5.445$$

Answer 5.445kg (or 5445g)

Test yourself

1. Jude bought a coffee for £1.40, a doughnut for £1.75 and an apple for 60p. What change did he get from £5?

2. Orange squash is made from 1 part squash concentrate and 5 parts water. If Poppy uses 150ml of squash concentrate, how many litres of orange squash does she make in total?

3. Jonny ran 2.5km on Monday, twice as far on Wednesday and four times as far on Friday. How far did he run in total?

4. The first four ingredients for a cake weigh 600g, 0.45kg, 150g and 0.15kg. The fifth ingredient takes the total weight to 1.5kg. How much did the fifth ingredient weigh?

Remember

If a measurement problem contains mixed units, change them so that they are all the same.

2-D shapes

2-D shapes are flat shapes. They are called 2-D because they have 2 dimensions: length (or height) and width. They have no depth.

When a 2-D shape has only straight sides it is known as a **polygon**.

Shapes and their properties

Circle: one curved side, with all points on the **circumference** the same distance from the centre.

Semicircle: half a circle, with one curved side and one straight side.

Triangles have three straight sides. There are different types of triangles:

- **equilateral triangle**: all the sides are of equal length and all the angles are equal

- **scalene triangle**: none of the sides are of equal length and none of the angles are equal

- **isosceles triangle**: two sides are of equal length and two of the angles are equal

- **right-angled triangle**: this can be an isosceles or scalene triangle, but must have a right angle.

Pentagon: five straight sides

Hexagon: six straight sides

Heptagon: seven straight sides

Octagon: eight straight sides

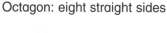

Other names you might come across:

- quadrilaterals: four straight sides (see page 69)
- nonagon: nine straight sides
- decagon: 10 straight sides
- dodecagon: 12 straight sides.

Test yourself

1. Cover up the definitions.
   Can you identify these shapes?
   a I have three sides of equal length and three equal angles.
   b None of my three sides are of equal length and none of my angles are equal.
   c I have five straight sides.
   d I have eight straight sides.

Remember

Triangle: three straight sides
Quadrilaterals: four straight sides
Pentagon: five straight sides
Hexagon: six straight sides
Heptagon: seven straight sides
Octagon: eight straight sides
Nonagon: nine straight sides
Decagon: 10 straight sides
Dodecagon: 12 straight sides

Quadrilaterals

All the shapes below are **quadrilaterals**. They all have four straight sides.

Parallelogram: two sets of parallel lines

Rectangle: four right angles – it is a type of parallelogram

Square: four right angles and four sides of equal length – it is a type of rectangle

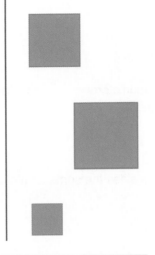

Rhombus: two sets of parallel lines and four sides of equal length – it is a type of parallelogram (a square is a special rhombus)

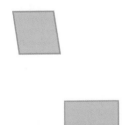

Trapezium: one set of parallel lines – one of the parallel lines is longer than the other

Kite: two short sides **adjacent** and of equal length, and two longer ones adjacent and of equal length

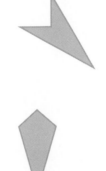

What about this shape?
It doesn't match any of the descriptions above, so is just called a quadrilateral.

Vertical lines go straight up and down.

Horizontal lines go from left to right.

Parallel lines are the same distance apart along their length.

Perpendicular lines are at right angles to each other.

Test yourself

1. What are these shapes?
   a I have four right angles and four sides of equal length.
   b I have one set of parallel lines.
2. Is this statement true?
   'A quadrilateral is always a parallelogram.'

Remember

Any shape with four equal sides is a quadrilateral. Most can also be described using more specific names, such as rhombus.

Regular and irregular shapes

All 2-D shapes are either regular or irregular.

Regular shapes

A regular shape has all its sides the same length and all its angles the same size, like these.

regular triangle
(**equilateral triangle**)

regular quadrilateral
(square)

regular pentagon

regular hexagon

Irregular shapes

An irregular shape does not have all its sides the same length and/or all its angles the same size.

irregular triangle
(not equal sides
or angles)

irregular quadrilateral
(not equal sides)

irregular pentagon
(not equal sides
or angles)

irregular hexagon
(not equal angles)

Congruent shapes

Shapes are **congruent** if they are identical in size and shape. They can be rotated, but must be the same size and have the same angles. These pairs of shapes are congruent.

Similar shapes

Shapes are similar if they have been made larger or smaller but have not changed their shape, like these.

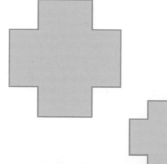

Test yourself

1. Cover up the definitions.Can you complete these sentences?
   a A regular shape has...   c Congruent shapes are...
   b An irregular shape...   d Similar shapes are...

Remember

A regular shape has all its sides the same length and all its angles the same size.

An irregular shape does not have all its sides the same length and/ or all its angles the same size.

3-D shapes

3-D shapes have 3 dimensions: length (or height), width and depth.

3-D shapes are also called three-dimensional or 'solid' shapes, even though they might be hollow.

Shapes with flat faces

Prism

A prism (such as a triangular prism, hexagonal prism or octagonal prism) has the same cross-section along its length. This cross-section can be any of the 2-D shapes. Think of a prism as a 2-D shape that has been stretched to make a 3-D shape.

cube	cuboid (rectangular prism)	triangular prism	pentagonal prism

Pyramid

A pyramid (such as a square-based pyramid or pentagonal-based pyramid) has a 2-D base, like a square, triangle or pentagon. The other **faces** are triangles and join together at a point or **vertex**.

square-based pyramid	triangular-based pyramid	pentagonal-based pyramid

Polyhedra

A 3-D shape with only flat faces is called a **polyhedron**. The shapes above are all polyhedra. Polyhedra are described by the number of faces they have.

- tetrahedron: a triangular-based pyramid with four faces
- hexahedron: a cube or cuboid with six faces
- octahedron: has eight flat faces

- decahedron: 10 flat faces
- dodecahedron: 12 flat faces
- icosahedron: 20 flat faces

Shapes with curved faces

The shapes below are not polyhedra as they have curved faces.

cylinder (circular prism)	cone	sphere	hemisphere

A coin is a 3-D shape and so is called a cylinder.

Test yourself

1. Cover up the text above, and name these shapes:

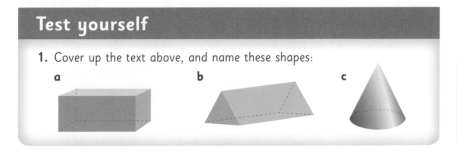

a   b   c

Remember

3-D shapes have three dimensions (length, width and height).
A polyhedron has only flat faces.

Properties of 3-D shapes

To describe 3-D shapes, you will need to know these words.

edge – where two faces meet

face – a flat or curved surface

vertex – a corner or point

Shape	Number of faces (F)	Number of vertices (V)	Number of edges (E)	
cube	6	8	12	polyhedra
cuboid	6	8	12	
triangular prism	5	6	9	
tetrahedron	4	4	6	
square-based pyramid	5	5	8	
cylinder	3	0	2	
cone	2	1	1	
sphere	1	0	0	
hemisphere	2	0	1	

Relationship between faces, vertices and edges

For all polyhedra (flat-faced shapes), the number of faces plus the number of vertices equals the number of edges plus 2.

$$F + V = E + 2$$

So, for example, for a cube: $6 + 8 = 12 + 2$

Nets

A **net** is what a 3-D shape would look like if it were opened out flat. Knowing the shapes of the faces within a 3-D shape will help you recognise (and draw) its net. The net for any particular 3-D shape can be drawn in a variety of ways.

Look at these examples of nets of cuboids, consisting of four identical rectangular faces and a further two identical rectangular faces.

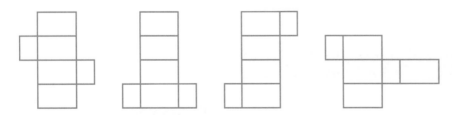

> ### Remember
>
> A cube has six faces, eight vertices, and 12 edges, and a cuboid has as well.
>
> $F + V = E + 2$

Test yourself

1. Complete these sentences.
   a A face is...
   b A vertex is...
   c An edge is...

2. Cover the table. How many faces, vertices and edges are there on these shapes?
   a cylinder
   b sphere
   c tetrahedron
   d cone
   e hemisphere
   f cuboid

3. Which 3-D shape is this the net of?

Transformations

Transformations are ways of changing or moving shapes.

You should know about three transformations: reflection, **rotation** and **translation**.

Reflection

To reflect a shape you need a mirror line, which might be horizontal, vertical or diagonal. The reflection or new shape is called the **image**. Watch what happens when the mirror line is diagonal.

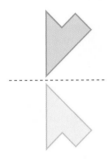
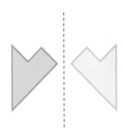

When reflecting a shape:

- take one **vertex** (corner) at a time

- look at where each is in relation to the mirror line – the image will be at the same point on the other side of the line.

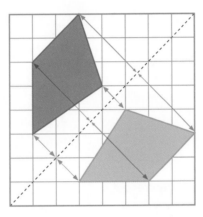

Remember

When reflecting a shape, take one vertex at a time. Turn the paper to make the mirror lines vertical if this helps.

Test yourself

1. Which picture shows a correct reflection of the red triangle in the dotted mirror line?

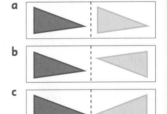

2. Give the co-ordinates of each vertex of the image of this shape when reflected in the mirror line.

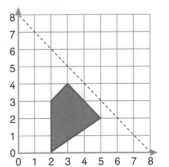

3. How many lines of symmetry are there in a regular hexagon?

Reflection symmetry

A shape has reflection symmetry when it has one or more lines of symmetry. These shapes all have reflection symmetry.

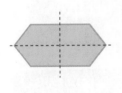

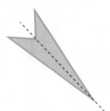
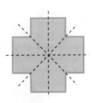

All regular shapes (see page 70) have the same number of lines of symmetry as number of sides, so an equilateral triangle has 3 sides and 3 lines of symmetry and a square has 4 sides and 4 lines of symmetry.

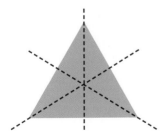
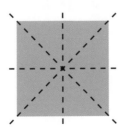

Rotational symmetry

A shape has **rotational symmetry** when it will fit into its outline in more than one way as it is turned through 360°. The number of times it fits is called the **order**. The shapes on the right all have rotational symmetry. All regular shapes have the same order of rotational symmetry as number of sides.

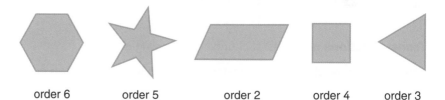

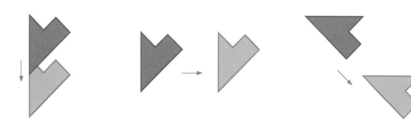

order 6   order 5   order 2   order 4   order 3

Translation

Translation means moving or sliding without turning. A translation can be vertical, horizontal or diagonal.

These shapes have been translated.

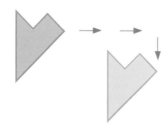

Diagonal translations are described by saying how many units across and how many units up or down the shape is moved.

This shape has been translated two to the right, and one down.

Translation and reflection

You may be asked to translate a shape and then reflect it.

Translate Shape A up 2 and right 3 then reflect it in the y axis. What are the coordinates of the reflected shape?

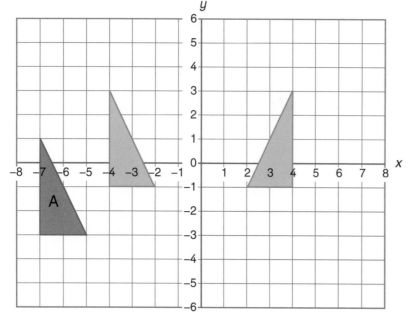

Answer (2,−1), (4,−1), (4,3)

Remember

A shape has rotational symmetry if it has an order of two or more. Translation means moving or sliding without turning.

Test yourself

1. What is the order of rotational symmetry of a regular octagon?

2. A rectangle has coordinates (−1,2), (−1,4), (3,4), (3,2). It is translated left 4 and down 3. What are its new coordinates?

3. It is then reflected in the y axis. What are the coordinates of the reflection?

Co-ordinates

Co-ordinates allow you to pinpoint exactly where a point or shape is on a graph or map. Co-ordinates are written in brackets separated by a comma, like this (5,12). They are an 'ordered pair' of numbers which means the order in which they are written is important.

the *x* co-ordinate → (5,12) ← the *y* co-ordinate

The first number shows how many places across to move on the horizontal **axis**.

The second number shows how many places up or down to move on the vertical axis.

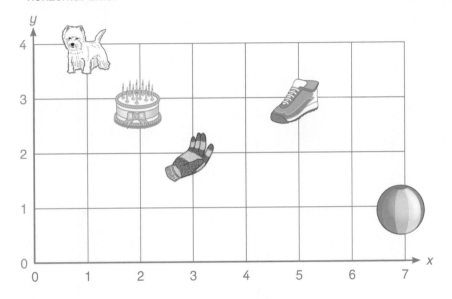

The cake is at (2,3), which means 2 across and 3 up.

The ball is at (7,1), which means 7 across and 1 up.

The trainer is at (5,3), which means 5 across and 3 up.

Drawing shapes with co-ordinates

You may be asked to plot several points, join them up and identify the shape you have drawn.

Plot these points: (0,1), (2,3), (4,1) and (6,3). What shape have you drawn?

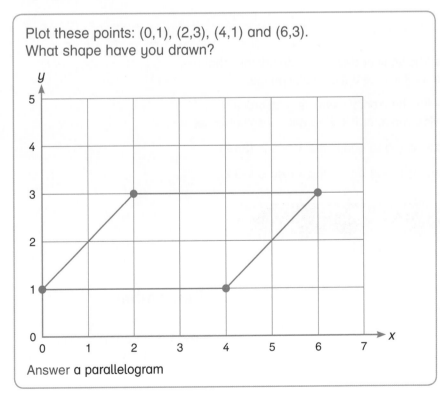

Answer **a parallelogram**

Remember

When plotting or reading co-ordinates, go across first, then up or down. Think: 'along the corridor then up or down the stairs'.

Test yourself

1. On the grid above, what are the co-ordinates of:
   a the dog
   b the glove?

2. Can you point to these co-ordinates?
   a (0,3)   **c** (3,4)
   b (3,0)   **d** (4,3)

3. Look at these co-ordinate sequences. Give three more co-ordinates that will lie along the same line.
   a (1,4), (2,7), (3,10), (4,13)
   b (3,6), (5,5), (7,4), (9,3)

Co-ordinates in all four quadrants

This grid has four **quadrants**. The 'first quadrant' in the grid has been coloured in.

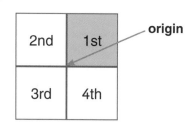

You can find the co-ordinates of points in all four quadrants by reading the **axes**, which run through the origin (centre point).

Only those points in the first quadrant have co-ordinates that are all positive. The other quadrants use **negative numbers** (see pages 9–11).

The origin of the graph is at (0,0).

The position of:

A is (3,2) B is (–2,2) C is (–3,–2)
D is (2,–4).

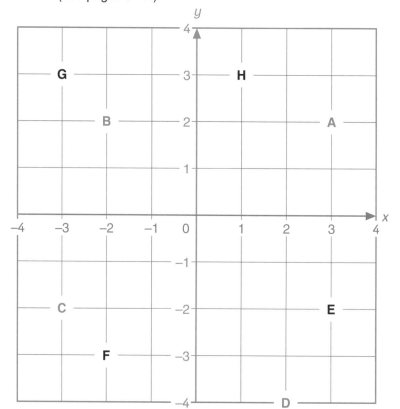

When a point is reflected in the **y axis** (the vertical axis), its *x* co-ordinate changes from positive to negative, or vice versa, or if it is zero it doesn't change.

When a point is reflected in the **x axis** (the horizontal axis), its *y* co-ordinate changes from positive to negative, or vice versa, or if it is zero it doesn't change.

A is at (3,2):   its reflection in the *y* axis is (–3,2) and in the *x* axis is (3,–2).

C is at (–3,–2): its reflection in the *y* axis is (3,–2) and in the *x* axis is (–3,2).

Test yourself

1. On the grid, what are the co-ordinates of letter:
   a E **b** F **c** G **d** H?

2. In which two quadrants are the *x* co-ordinates always negative?

3. In which two quadrants are the *y* co-ordinates always negative?

4. In which quadrant are the *x* and *y* co-ordinates always negative?

5. Write the co-ordinates of point G when reflected in:
   a the *y* axis **b** the *x* axis.

Remember

The *x* axis is horizontal (across), the *y* axis is vertical (up and down). Think: '*x* is a cross (across), *y* is high'.

Working out co-ordinates using other co-ordinates

If you are given the **co-ordinates** of a shape and asked to find the co-ordinates of one of its **vertices** (corners), you don't always need to draw a grid. Look at this example.

A square has vertices at these three co-ordinates: (4,3) (4,0) (7,0). What are the co-ordinates of the fourth vertex?

First sketch the square.

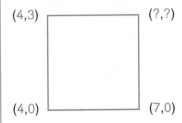

(4,3)   (?,?)

(4,0)   (7,0)

Notice that the *x* co-ordinates of points above or below one another are the same.

4 and 4 are on the same vertical line

7 and ? are on the same vertical line

Notice that the *y* co-ordinates of points along the same horizontal line are the same.

0 and 0 are along the same horizontal line

3 and ? are along the same horizontal line

Answer the missing co-ordinate is (7,3)

Co-ordinates along straight lines

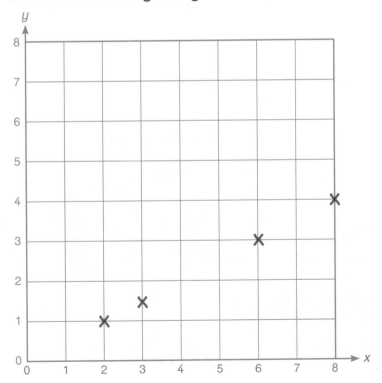

When any straight line is drawn on a grid, patterns in the co-ordinates can be found. In the grid above, the co-ordinates of points along a straight line follow this pattern: the *x* co-ordinate is always twice the *y* co-ordinate. All these points lie along the same straight line.

(2,1)   (3,1.5)   (6,3)   (8,4)

Remember

The *x* co-ordinates of points above or below each other are the same.

The *y* co-ordinates of points in the same horizontal line are the same.

Test yourself

1. A square has vertices at (6,6) (6,2) (10,2). What are the co-ordinates of the fourth vertex?

2. A square has vertices at (4,6) (4,1) (9,1). What are the co-ordinates of the fourth vertex?

3. The pattern of some co-ordinates along a straight line is: the *x* co-ordinate is always 3 more than the *y* co-ordinate. Write four co-ordinates.

Angles

An angle is an amount of turn measured in degrees. Each angle is a fraction of a whole turn. Degrees, shown with the symbol °, are an accurate way of showing the amount of turn.

There are 360 degrees in a full turn, written 360°.

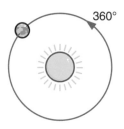   

$\frac{1}{4}$ or 90° turn $\frac{1}{2}$ or 180° turn $\frac{3}{4}$ or 270° turn

Instead of an arrow showing the turn, use an **arc**.

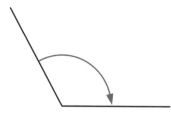 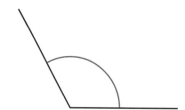

Types of angle

An angle less than 90° is called an **acute** angle.

An angle of 90° is called a right angle.

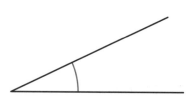 

An angle between 90° and 180° is called an **obtuse** angle.

An angle of 180° is called a straight angle.

An angle between 180° and 360° is called a **reflex** angle.

Test yourself

1. Cover up the text on this page. Can you remember the names of each of these?
   a an angle of 90°
   b an angle of 180°
   c an angle between 180° and 360°
   d an angle between 90° and 180°
   e an angle less than 90°

2. What type of angle am I?
   a I'm 67°
   b I'm 328°
   c I'm 180°
   d I'm 100°
   e I'm 90°
   f I'm 297°
   g I'm 21°

Remember

Acute: less than 90°
Right: 90°
Obtuse: between 90° and 180°
Straight: 180°
Reflex: between 180° and 360°

Angles in shapes

You might be asked to identify angles in shapes.

How many acute, right, obtuse and reflex angles can you find inside this shape?

a obtuse   d reflex   g reflex

b acute   e acute   h acute

c reflex   f right   i obtuse

Answer acute 3, right 1, obtuse 2, reflex 3

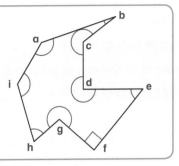

Measuring angles

A protractor (sometimes called an angle measurer) is used to measure the size of an angle.

How to use a protractor

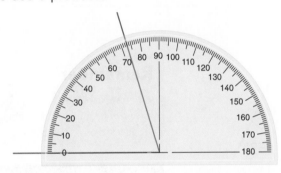

1. Line up the centre with the point where the two lines meet.

2. Turn the protractor until one of the lines is along the zero line.

3. Count around from zero, in tens, until you reach the other line.

4. Read the scale carefully.

To measure a reflex angle, measure the acute angle and subtract that from 360°.

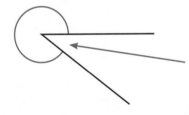

The acute angle is 38° therefore the reflex angle must be 360° − 38° = 322°.

Remember

If the angle is acute, it will be smaller than 90°. If the angle is obtuse, it will be between 90° and 180°.

Sometimes you might have to extend the lines with a pencil and ruler to help you use the protractor.

Test yourself

1. How many acute, right, obtuse and reflex angles can you find inside this shape?

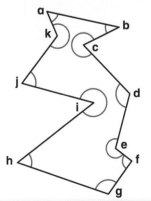

2. Measure these angles:

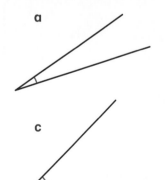

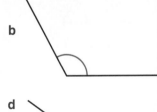

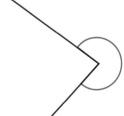

Drawing angles

How to draw an angle of 63°

1. Draw a straight line.

2. Place your protractor so that:

   - the central cross is at one end of the line
   - the zero line lies on top of your line.

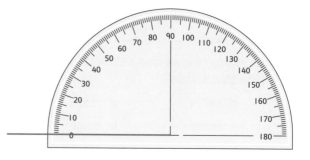

3. Count around from 0° and make a mark at 63°.

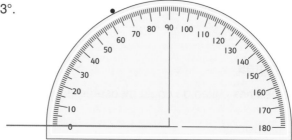

4. Remove your protractor and draw a line from the dot to the end of your line.

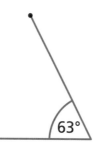

63°

To draw a reflex angle, work out the associated acute angle by subtracting from 360° and use the protracter to draw that.

Estimating angles

You might be asked to estimate the size of angles without using a protractor, as below.

Estimate the size of these angles

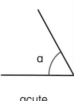

a

acute

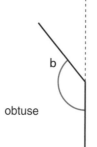

b

obtuse

First of all, decide on the type of each angle.

Angle a is acute, so it is between 0° and 90°.

Answer angle a is about 60°

Angle b is obtuse – between 90° and 180°.

Answer angle b is about 140°

Remember

When measuring, drawing or estimating angles, think about what type of angle it is first.

Test yourself

1. Draw angles of:

a 30°	d 125°
b 45°	e 168°
c 80°	f 224°

2. Estimate, then measure, the size of these angles.

   a

   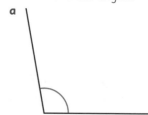

   b

   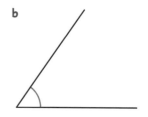

   c

Calculating angles

There are many types of angle question where you are expected to **calculate**, rather than measure, the size of missing angles.

Angles in a triangle

The three inside angles of a triangle add up to 180°.

You can prove this by tearing a triangle into three pieces, with a corner in each.

Join the corners together to make a straight line. You know there are 180° in a straight angle, so there must be 180° in a triangle.

Find the missing angle

65° + 60° = 125°

180° − 125° = 55°

Check: 65° + 60° + 55° = 180°

Answer 55°

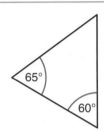

Angles at a point

Find the missing reflex angle

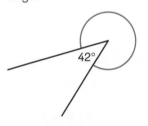

There are 360° in a full turn.

360° − 42° = 318°

Check: 318° + 42° = 360°

Answer 318°

Angles on a straight line

Find the missing angle

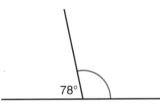

There are 180° in a straight angle.

180° − 78° = 102°

Check: 78° + 102° = 180°

Answer 102°

Vertically opposite angles

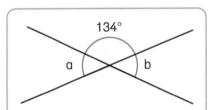

When two lines cross, the opposite angles are always equal.

180° − 134° = 46° so a = 46°

If a = 46°, then b = 46°

Answer 46°

Test yourself

1. Find the missing angle.

2. Find the missing angle.

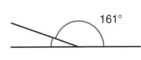

3. Find the missing angle.

Remember

There are 360° in a full turn and 180° in a straight angle.

The angles in a triangle add up to 180°.

Angles in polygons

The angles inside a triangle always add up to 180°.

$$a + b + c = 180°$$

The angles inside a **quadrilateral** always add up to 360°.

$$d + e + f + g = 360°$$

The angles inside a pentagon always add up to 540°.

The angles inside a hexagon always add up to 720°.

Notice that the number of degrees follows a pattern. It goes up by 180° for each extra side on a **polygon**.

Number of sides	3	4	5	6	7	8
Number of degrees	180	360	540	720	900	1080

If a shape is regular all its angles are equal, so you can find the size of one angle in regular shapes.

- For a regular (**equilateral**) triangle each angle is: 180° ÷ 3 = 60°
- For a regular quadrilateral (square) each angle is: 360° ÷ 4 = 90°
- For a regular pentagon each angle is: 540° ÷ 5 = 108°
- For a regular hexagon each angle is: 720° ÷ 6 = 120° and so on.

Remember

The angles in a quadrilateral add up to 360°. Each shape with one more side has angles totalling 180° more than the last.

Calculate angle y in this pentagon

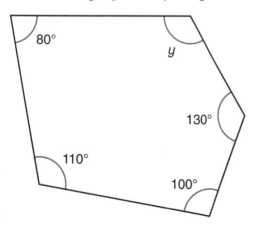

Add the known angles
100 + 130 + 110 + 80
= 420

Subtract from the total number of degrees in a pentagon

540 − 420 = 120

Answer **angle y is 120°**

Test yourself

1. What size is each angle in a regular octagon?

2. A quadrilateral has angles of 70°, 130°, 80° and m. Find angle m.

3. An isosceles triangle has two angles of 70°. What is the third angle?

4. What is the total number of degrees of the angles inside a 9-sided polygon (nonagon)?

Circles

Make sure you learn the special words related to the lines and edges of circles.

The **radius** is the distance from the edge to the centre of the circle. It is half the size of the **diameter**, which is the widest distance across the circle, through the centre.

The **circumference** is another word for the **perimeter** of the circle. Part of the circumference is called an **arc**.

radius

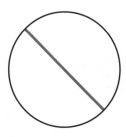

diameter

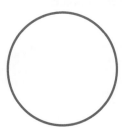

circumference

arc

Here are some other circle words you can learn.

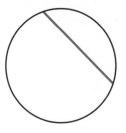

chord

segment

sector

How long is the radius of a circle that has a diameter of 30 cm?

 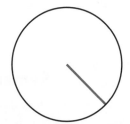

The radius is half the length of the diameter so the radius is half of 30cm. 30cm ÷ 2 = 15cm

Answer 15cm

Test yourself

1. Which of these words describes the perimeter of a circle: chord, circumference or sector?

2. What is the name of the line from one side of a circle to the other, passing through the centre of the circle?

3. If the radius of a circle is 5cm, what is its diameter?

4. A circle has a circumference of 30cm. An arc is marked on the circle that is one-sixth of the length of the circumference. What is the length of the arc?

Remember

Diameter is a longer word than radius, and the diameter of a circle is longer than its radius – it is always twice as long.

Handling data

Frequency tables

A **frequency** table shows us how often something happens or how many things we have.
To record data you can use tallying, where you group data in fives, like this: ⃫ = 5.
You then write the frequency (or total) alongside. These tables are also known as tally charts.

A frequency table showing how many birds visited the bird table in one hour

Type	Tally	Frequency
Blackbird	⃫	5
Robin	II	2
Sparrow	⃫ II	7
Magpie	IIII	4
Greenfinch	⃫ IIII	9

Pictograms

This information can also be shown on a pictogram, like the one on the right. Symbols or pictures are used to show one or more items. Always give your pictogram a key and a title.

A pictogram showing how many birds visited the bird table in one hour

Bar graphs

Bar graphs, like other graphs, show information, or data, as a picture to make it more easily understood. Always label each **axis** and give your graph a title.

A bar graph showing how many birds visited the bird table in one hour

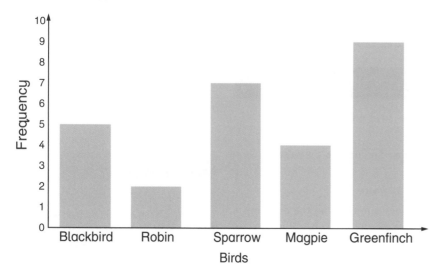

Remember

When drawing a graph, make sure you always label each axis and give the graph a title.

Test yourself

1. Draw a frequency table of this data, using tallying. Shoe size of children in a class:
   13, 1, 13, 12, 2, 12, 1, 1, 2, 1, 12, 12, 4, 13, 13, 12, 1, 2, 1, 1, 13, 13, 1, 12, 1, 13, 2, 4
   (Your total should be 28.)

2. Draw a bar graph of the data in question 1.

Grouped data

Bar charts can also show **grouped data**. This is data that has been grouped together to make it easier to show.

The birthday months of a group of 11-year-olds

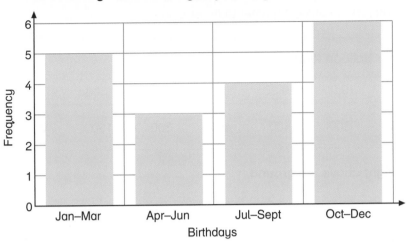

If this data wasn't grouped you would need 12 separate columns, one for each month. The data is called **discrete data** because it is about things you can count, like the number of people with a birthday between January and March.

When you count the number of people with a birthday between January and March, you are finding the **frequency**.

Bar line graphs

This bar line graph uses bar lines to show the same information.

The birthday months of a group of 11-year-olds

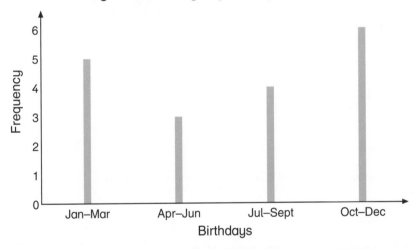

Test yourself

1. Use the graphs to find:
   a the number of 11-year-olds with a birthday between April and June
   b how many more 11-year-olds had a birthday in October to December than in July to September
   c the total number of 11-year-olds surveyed.

2. Is it true that more of this group of 11-year-olds have a birthday in November than in May? Explain your answer.

Remember

Data which has been grouped together is often easier to show in a graph.

Line graphs

Line graphs are a way of showing what is happening over a period of time. The data is called **continuous data** because it is about things that can be measured. You write time on the horizontal **axis**. You then plot the data and join the points together to make a line.

Here is some information about a hot air balloon flight during an evening

Time	18:00	18:30	19:00	19:30	20:00	20:30	21:00	21:30
Balloon's height above ground (metres)	0	250	300	400	450	300	150	0

A line graph to show a balloon's height above the ground

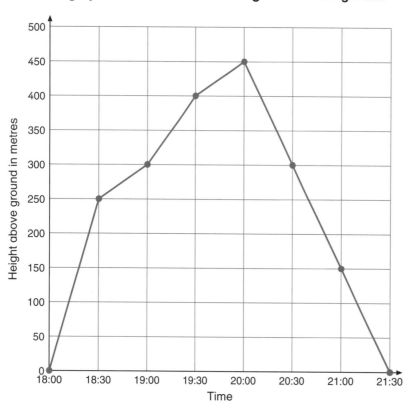

For how long was the balloon above 300m?

On the graph, find when the balloon first rose above 300m (19:00) and then when it dropped below it (20:30).

Answer **It was above 300m for 1 hour and a half.**

Test yourself

1. At what time did the balloon first rise to:
   a 250m   **b** 400m?

2. On its descent, when did the balloon drop to:
   a 300m   **b** 150m?

3. At about what time was the balloon at:
   a 50m   **b** 275m?

4. Could the balloon have gone any higher than 450m? Why?

Remember

When answering questions about line graphs, be careful to read across and down from the points accurately.

Pie charts

A pie chart shows information as different-sized **sectors** of a circle.

Pie charts are useful for showing **proportions** of a whole, like what fraction of your money you spend on different things, or how you spend your time.

These pie charts show how Daisy and Megan spent their free time last Saturday. What fraction of their free time did each girl spend on each activity?

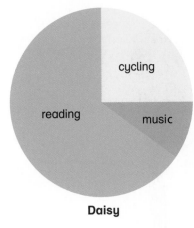

Daisy

Megan

Answer

Daisy spent: about two-thirds of her time reading
about one-quarter cycling
about one-tenth listening to music

Megan spent: half her time shopping
about one-quarter visiting friends
about one-eighth watching TV
about one-eighth cooking

If Megan had eight hours of free time last Saturday, how long did she spend on each activity?

Shopping: half of 8 hours = 4 hours
Answer 4 hours

Visiting friends: about one-quarter of 8 hours = about 2 hours
Answer 2 hours

Watching TV: about one-eighth of 8 hours = about 1 hour
Answer 1 hour

Cooking: about one-eighth of 8 hours = about 1 hour
Answer 1 hour

Test yourself

1. What fraction of each circle is blue?

  a   b   c   d

Remember

Look carefully to see what fraction of the circle is shaded in a pie chart.

Drawing pie charts

To draw pie charts you need to find what angle the sector (slice) for each category will be. First divide 360° by the total number of people or items that the pie chart will represent. Then multiply your answer by how many there are in each category.

angle for one item = 360° ÷ the total number of things represented

This table shows the activities or items that 60 boys spend the largest part of their pocket money on. Draw a pie chart to illustrate this.

Activity or item	Number of boys
Sports and hobbies	25
Clothes	12
Music, videos, films	10
Computer games	8
Other	5

The total number of boys is 60. Divide 360° by 60 to show the angle for each boy.

360° ÷ 60 = 6°

Then multiply this angle by the number of boys in each category.

Sports and hobbies	6 × 25 = 150°
Clothes	6 × 12 = 72°
Music, video and films	6 × 10 = 60°
Computer games	6 × 8 = 48°
Other	6 × 5 = 30°

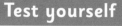

Test yourself

1. Find the angles of each sector in the pie chart for each item in this table, representing 30 boys.

Activity or item	Number of boys
Sports and hobbies	8
Clothes	7
Music, videos, films	6
Computer games	5
Other	4

2. Now draw a pie chart to show the information in the table.

Remember

Remember to check that all your angles add up to 360°.

Mean average

The **mean** is a type of **average** that gives an idea of a whole set of values.

This list of numbers shows how many texts Leo sent on five different days. Find the mean number of texts sent.

10 2 7 9 2

To find the mean, find the total of all the values and divide by the number of values.

$10 + 2 + 7 + 9 + 2 = 30$

$30 \div 5$ values $= 6$

Answer 6

This list shows the number of calls Ella made on 10 different days. Find the mean number of calls made.

17 15 11 10 9 12 13 19 10 19

The mean is 13.5.

$17 + 15 + 11 + 10 + 9 + 12 + 13 + 19 + 10 + 19 = 135$

$135 \div 10 = 13.5$

Notice that the mean doesn't have to be a whole number!

Answer 13.5

Test yourself

1. Find the mean. 6 8 2 1 8 3 7
2. The mean of these cards is 6. What is the missing number?

   6   5   9   4   ☐

3. The mean of these cards is 7. What is the missing number?

   1   8   5   8   ☐

4. This spreadsheet shows the amounts Kareem earned from jobs over six months. Find the mean.

	A	B
1	Jan	£115
2	Feb	£125
3	Mar	£180
4	Apr	£153
5	May	£115
6	Jun	£119

Remember

An average is one value that gives you an idea of a whole set of values. To find the mean, add the values together, then divide by the number of values.

Answers

Page 4

1 a *300 + 10 + 2*

  b 4000 + 800 + 30 + 9

  c 60 000 + 9000 + 200 + 10 + 5

  d 2 000 000 + 100 000 + 6000 + 300 + 80 + 7

2 a 2 (or two)

  b 20 (or twenty)

  c 200 (or two hundred)

  d 20 000 (or twenty thousand)

  e 200 000 (or two hundred thousand)

  f 2 000 000 (or two million)

Page 5

1 a three hundred and fifty-one

  b four thousand, eight hundred and fifty-seven

  c two thousand and forty-one

  d fifty thousand and ninety-one

  e six hundred and fifty-nine thousand, two hundred and thirty-four

  f two million, four hundred and thirty-seven thousand, eight hundred and ninety-six

2 a 5254

  b 61 591

  c 6 504 308

Page 7

1 a 2420

  b 3500

  c 5430

  d 6500

2 a 2900

  b 8600

  c 9000

  d 63 000

3 a 62 000

  b 45 000

  c 75 000

  d 40 000

4 a 4 740 000, 4 700 000, 5 000 000

  b 2 890 000, 2 900 000, 3 000 000

  c 6 190 000, 6 200 000, 6 000 000

Page 8

1 92 716, 80 062, 67 293, 8502, 6291

2 48 602, 48 701, 50 001, 51 762, 54 351

3 3 163 067, 3 461 590, 3 491 042, 3 493 533, 3 946 724

4 3323

Page 9

1 a 3

  b −2

  c −9

  d −5

  e −14

  f −10

Page 10

1 a −2, 0, 4, 6, 7

  b −9, −1, 2, 3, 4

  c −7, −4, −2, 4, 10

  d −15, −5, −2, −1, 7

  e −54, −23, −12, −6, −1

2 a 8°C

  b 13°C

Page 11

1 a 7

  b 12

  c 9

  d 5

  e 9

2 a −7

  b −8

  c −8

  d −11

  e −12

  f −12

3 a −1

  b −1

  c 4

  d 7

  e 2

  f −2

Page 12

1 a 32, 39, 46…

  b 43, 52, 61…

  c 17, 11, 5…

  d 4, −9, −22…

2 a 19, 25, 32…

  b 27, 37, 49…

  c 14, 7, −1…

  d 62, 55, 49…

3 Explanations of patterns such as:

  1a The sequence starts with the number 4 and each term in the sequence increases by a difference of 7 each time.

  1b The sequence starts with the number 7 and each term in the sequence increases by a difference of 9 each time.

  1c The sequence starts with the number 41 and each term in the sequence decreases by a difference of 6 each time.

  1d The sequence starts with the number 56 and each term in the sequence decreases by a difference of 13 each time.

  2a This increasing sequence starts with the number 5 and the differences between each term increase by 1 each time. The difference goes 2, 3, 4, 5… and so on.

  2b This increasing sequence starts with the number 7 and the differences between each term increase by 2 each time. The difference goes 2, 4, 6, 8… and so on.

  2c This decreasing sequence starts with the number 32 and the differences between each term increase by 1 each time. The difference goes 3, 4, 5, 6… and so on.

  2d This decreasing sequence starts with the number 100 and the differences between each term decrease by 1 each time. The difference goes 11, 10, 9, 8… and so on.

Page 13

1 a (2), 7, 12, 17, (22)

  b (3) 11, 19, 27, (35)

  c (24), 18, 12, 6, (0)

  d (1), 6, 11, 16, (21)

  e (36), 29, 22, 15, (8)

2 a (8), 6, 4, 2, 0, (−2)

  b (−3), 1, 5, 9, 13, (17)

  c (21), 11, 1, −9, (−19)

  d (−3), −7, −11, −15, −19, (−23)

  e (32), 20, 8, (−4)

Page 14

1 a 350 000, 3 500 000, 35 000 000… (×10)

  b 5184, 31 104, 186 624… (×6)

2 a 6, 3, 1.5… (÷2)

  b 0.000246, 0.00000246, 0.0000000246… (÷100)

  c $\frac{7}{9}$, $\frac{8}{9}$, 1 $(+\frac{1}{9})$

3 a 50, 500, 5000

  b 640, 6400, 64 000

  c 870, 8700, 87 000

  d 2380, 23 800, 238 000

  e 5340, 53 400, 534 000

  f 6970, 69 700, 697 000

4 a 600, 60, 6

  b 720, 72, 7.2

  c 6900, 690, 69

  d 126.4, 12.64, 1.264

  e 650.3, 65.03, 6.503

  f 1100.1, 110.01, 11.001

Page 15

1 a 68, 140

  b 18, 19

  c 55, 111

Page 16

1 1067

2 a XLVII

  b DXCIII

  c MV

  d MMCXLIV

3 a 76

  b 228

  c 1961

Page 17

1 a $\frac{5}{8}$

  b $\frac{3}{4}$

  c $\frac{3}{9}$ or $\frac{1}{3}$

2 a $\frac{1}{2}$

  b $\frac{2}{5}$

  c $\frac{1}{4}$

  d $\frac{2}{3}$

  e $\frac{7}{10}$

  f $\frac{3}{4}$

Page 18

1 a, c, d, e

2 a $\frac{1}{4}$

  b $\frac{5}{6}$

  c $\frac{4}{11}$

  d $\frac{5}{7}$

Schofield & Sims